J. Moyr Smith

Ancient Greek Female Costume

J. Moyr Smith

Ancient Greek Female Costume

ISBN/EAN: 9783337005733

Printed in Europe, USA, Canada, Australia, Japan

Cover: Foto ©Thomas Meinert / pixelio.de

More available books at **www.hansebooks.com**

This

... is an authorized facsimile made from a microfilm copy of the original book. Further unauthorized copying is prohibited.

Books on Demand is a publishing service of UMI. The program offers xerographic reprints of more than 130,000 books that are no longer in print. Some titles are also available on microfilm.

The primary focus of Books on Demand is academic and professional resource materials originally published by university presses, academic societies, and trade book publishers worldwide.

This on-demand reprint was reproduced from microfilm by printing each page on a continuous roll of paper. Since only one side of the sheet is printed, it is folded to give the appearance of having printing on both sides. It does, however, result in odd-numbered pages being in the left-hand position rather than in the right-hand position. Printed text and line-drawing illustrations reproduce well from microfilm. Half-tones (photographs) generally do not reproduce well.

U·M·I
BOOKS ON DEMAND

University Microfilms International
A Bell & Howell Company
300 North Zeeb Road
P.O. Box 1346
Ann Arbor, Michigan 48106-1346
1-800-521-0600   313-761-4700

Printed in 1994 by xerographic process on acid-free paper

ANCIENT
GREEK FEMALE COSTUME.

ILLUSTRATED

BY

ONE HUNDRED AND TWELVE PLATES
AND NUMEROUS SMALLER ILLUSTRATIONS.

WITH EXPLANATORY LETTERPRESS, AND DESCRIPTIVE PASSAGES
FROM THE WORKS OF HOMER, HESIOD, HERODOTUS,
ÆSCHYLUS, EURIPIDES, ARISTOPHANES, THEOCRITUS, XENOPHON,
LUCIAN, AND OTHER GREEK AUTHORS,

SELECTED BY

J. MOYR SMITH.

London:
SAMPSON LOW, MARSTON, SEARLE, & RIVINGTON,
CROWN BUILDINGS, 188, FLEET STREET.
1882.
[All rights reserved.]

LONDON:
PRINTED BY GILBERT AND RIVINGTON, LIMITED,
ST. JOHN'S SQUARE.

Reproduced by

DUOPAGE PROCESS

in the

U.S. of America

Micro Photo Division
Bell & Howell Company
Cleveland, Ohio 44112

PREFACE.

A GOOD many people of fair culture, if asked their opinion of Greek costume, would say that correct Greek costume seemed to consist chiefly of a pair of sandals for the feet, and a ribbon for the hair. In some of the most popular and best known works of Greek art there is even less dress than this. The Venus de Medici has not even a pair of sandals. The statues called the Theseus, the Discobulus, the Laöcoön are as bare of clothing, and though the Apollo Belvidere is furnished with a cloak, he does not use it to enshroud his limbs. The popular belief that ancient Greek costume was scarcely appreciable in quantity has thus some apparent foundation in fact. When the question is pressed still further, however, we begin to remember that the Caryatides of the Erechtheion, and the goddess Athénè, have each a distinctive dress covering the whole body, and that several of the female deities, such as Hèrè, Cybelè, and Artemis, are scarcely, if ever, represented unclothed.

This limited wardrobe is, however, nearly all that was credited to the Greeks by many people who were far from being ignorant of Greek art and Greek literature.

When, however, we come to study Greek literature

and Greek art with a view to costume, we are amazed at the richness and diversity for which Greek dresses were distinguished. In literature, Homer is full of allusions to magnificent dresses; and the paintings on vases supply us with hundreds of realistic representations of costumes which were undoubtedly taken from models in daily life.

To account for this seeming discrepancy we must call to mind that the most popular Greek statues nearly all belong to one period of Hellenic art, and that these statues were the product of a time when sculptural art had reached its zenith. As the human form unclothed gave the sculptor a fairer opportunity of showing his transcendent abilities—the mastery of form and the rendering of flesh being more difficult than the sculpture of drapery—he naturally chose subjects on which the dress was scanty and the limbs well displayed.

Representations of nude figures do occur in archaic sculpture and pottery, but they are chiefly bacchanalian subjects; and, as a rule, the figures in early examples are all dressed. Aphroditè (Venus) is clothed, and Heraclés is everywhere seen wearing the spoils of the Nemean lion. But no sculptural models of these were made, they were seldom photographed, and rarely seen; when seen they were passed over with a smile at their quaint inartistic stiffness, and scarcely admitted by the purists to be Greek art at all. Hence, in spite of the teeming examples of

PREFACE. 5

varied costumes exhibited on the Greek vases, and in early statues and bas-reliefs, ordinary culture persisted in recognizing as Greek only the works of the age of Phidias, or works which followed the usages of the Phidian period of sculpture.

Though I have been interested in Greek costume for many years, it was only comparatively recently that I discovered that such a book as Hope's "Costumes of the Ancients" existed. It was a revelation of the diversity, beauty, fitness, and grace of the early Greek dress, and also showed that culture, research, and enterprise at the beginning of this century were well directed.

It is from this book, published in 1812, and from Müller's "Denkmäler," that the plates and some of the cuts in the letterpress have been taken. To render the work more complete, various other illustrations have been added; these have been drawn direct from the paintings on ancient vases in the British Museum and the Louvre.

In the arrangement of the plates I have not been guided entirely by chronological sequence, but have rather endeavoured to group figures with similar kinds of dresses together; so that the artist or decorative draughtsman who wishes to make use of the book may find various dresses of the same kind with the least possible trouble.

In the letterpress I have generally retained the usual Latinized form of spelling Greek proper names, though I am aware there is at present a taste for the original

Greek form. But in a work that appeals not to scholars but to lovers of art, it would probably only lead to confusion were the reader to find the familiar Circe, Cyclades, Sicily, and Thrace under the forms of Kirkê, Kuklades, Sikania or Sikelia, and Thrakia. Moreover, those who have attempted to reform our spelling in this respect have usually carried out their improvements in a very imperfect way. In some instances that I have seen, one half of a name has the Greek form, and the other half is in the familiar Latinized form. Nor do I think that those people who spell Pheidias for Phidias and Phoibos for Phœbus will do Greek any great service by this display of scholarship while the ridiculous English style of pronouncing Greek is retained; the popular pronunciation of Phœbus is much nearer the Greek original than the popular English pronunciation of Phoibos would be. When, however, the Latin name is so altered as to be entirely different from the Greek, I sometimes use the Greek name in preference to the Latin one, as Aphroditè for Venus, Athéuè for Minerva, and Odysseus for Ulysses:

Fig. 1. Dorian or Early Greek Costume.

ANCIENT GREEK FEMALE COSTUME.

Fig. 2. Nausicaa and her Maids.—Od. vi.

ANCIENT Greece in its prime was much larger than the modern kingdom. Besides Attica and the peninsula of the Morea, or Peloponnesus, with its districts of Achaia, Elis, Arcadia, Argolis, Laconia, and Messenia, it included a great portion of country lying to the north of the Gulf of Corinth, which was inhabited by the Acarnians, Ætolians, Locrians, Phocians, Bœotians, Thessalians, and other tribes. At one time it extended to and included Macedonia and the countries lying to the north of the Ægean Sea. To this extensive country were to be added the islands of Crete, Rhodes, Euboea, and the numerous others lying to the east and west of the Peloponnesus, as well as those of Lesbos, Samos, and Chios, that adjoined Asia Minor. These together formed what might be called Greece proper; but Greece also possessed the colonies of Ionia, Æolis, Lycia, Cyprus, and other territories of Asia Minor on the east, and Sicily and Southern Italy on the west. The last was called Magna Græcia, because the colony outstripped the mother country in size, in the same way that America or Larger Britain outstrips the England of to-day.

But Greek influence was by no means confined to Greece and its colonies; and the strength of that influence in foreign countries may be gauged by the fact that a people like the Jews, so tenacious of their own customs, names, and traditions, adopted Greek for their written language, discarded their old Hebrew names, and called themselves by such Hellenic appellations as Jason, Antigonus, and Antipater.

In the time of Homer there was no general appellation for the Grecian race, the term Ἕλληνες (Hellénes) being one of later origin. The poet, therefore, when he wishes to designate the Greeks collectively, employs the name of the principal tribe, or the one he most favoured, as in the opening lines of the Iliad,—

"Μῆνιν ἄειδε θεά, Πηληϊάδεω Ἀχιλῆος
Οὐλομένην ἣ μυρί' Ἀχαιοῖς ἄλγε' ἔθηκεν,"

where Achaiois or Achæans is used for the Greek race. But in ordinary cases the inhabitants of each tract of country are discriminated by distinctive appellations, as

Argives, Laconians or Spartans, Arcadians, Samians, Lesbians, Æginetæ, and so on. This custom was usual in the time of Herodotus and Xenophon, and still later, and was rendered necessary by the fact that each of these petty states, though belonging to the Amphictyonic council, was governed by its own laws, had its distinctive customs, and approved costumes. In this extensive country, so varied by fertile plains, forest-covered hills, bleak mountainous districts, and rock-bound islands, an infinite variety of costumes existed at one and the same time, and probably one district borrowed from another in such a way that what was the prevailing manner in one country or island at one time, was superseded by another fashion borrowed from another district. This is mentioned so that when a seeming contradiction occurs, the reader may understand that the one remark applies to one part of Greece, and the other to a different part, or to the same part at a later time. These changes will perhaps be better understood if we quote an incident from Herodotus, relating to a dispute between the Argians and the Lacedæmonians about a tract of country called Thyrea. It was stipulated that the main body of each army should withdraw to its own country, and that 300 men on each side should engage. "They fought with such equal success, that of the 600, three men only were left alive—of the Argians, Alcenor and Chronius, and of the Lacedæmonians, Othryades; these survived when night came on. The two Argians, thinking themselves victorious, ran to Argos with the news; but Othryades, the Lacedæmonian, having stripped the corpses of the Argians, and carried their arms to his own camp, continued at his post. On the next day both armies, being informed of the event, met again in the same place; and for a time both laid claim to the victory—the one side alleging that the greater number of their men survived; the other side urging that those survivors had fled, and that their countryman had kept the field and spoiled their dead. At length, from words they betook themselves to blows; and when many had fallen on both sides, the Lacedæmonians obtained the victory. From that time the Argians, cutting off their hair, which they had before been compelled to wear long, enacted a law, which was confirmed by a curse, that no Argian should suffer his hair to grow, nor any woman wear ornaments of gold, till they should recover Thyrea. On the other hand, the Lacedæmonians made a contrary law, enjoining all their people to wear long hair, which they had never done before." Nor were these differences by any means confined to the men; for while in one part of Greece women were strictly confined to their own apartments, did not meet the guests at an entertainment given in the house, and were not permitted to go beyond the outer door, in another district more than modern English freedom was allowed them.

In one place women who had no husbands, whether virgins or widows, were strictly looked after—especially the virgins, as being less experienced—and they were rarely permitted to appear in public or converse with men; and when allowed that liberty, wore over their faces a veil, which was termed καλύπτρον or καλύπτρα, and which was not left off in public till the third day after marriage.

SPARTAN FEMALE COSTUME.

But in Laconia the Lacedæmonian or Spartan women observed fashions quite different from all their neighbours; their virgins went abroad bare-faced, the married women were covered with veils; the former designing (as Charilaus replied to one that inquired the reason of that custom) to get themselves husbands, whereas the latter aimed at nothing more than keeping those they already had.

Fig. 3.

Lycurgus, the Spartan lawgiver, seems to have encouraged a fashion in the younger women of wearing exceeding scanty costume, and even accustomed the virgins to dance and sing unclothed in the presence of the young men in the national festivals. There they indulged in raillery of the youths who had misbehaved themselves, and praised those who had distinguished themselves by their bravery or address in the games, thus exciting in

Fig. 4. Spartan Virgin.

the young men an emulation and love of glory. By wearing the scanty garment, or none at all, the Spartan girls had freedom in the exercises of running, wrestling, and throwing quoits and darts, and their bodies became strong and vigorous. "As for the virgins appearing naked," says Plutarch, "there was nothing disgraceful in it, because everything was conducted with modesty and without one indecent word or action, nay, it caused a simplicity of manners and an emulation for the best habit of body; their ideas, too, were naturally enlarged, while they were not excluded from their share of bravery and honour. Hence they were furnished with sentiments and language such as Gorgê, the wife of Leonidas, is said to have made use of when a woman of another country said to her, 'You of Lacedæmon are the only women in the world who rule the men.' She answered, 'We are the only women that bring forth men.'"

In another place, however, Plutarch says Numa's strictness as to virgins tended to form them to that modesty which is the ornament of their sex; but the great liberty which Lycurgus gave them, brought upon them the censure of the poets, particularly Ibycus; for they call them *Phænomerides* and *Andromaneis*. Euripides describes them in this manner:—

> "These quit their homes, ambitious to display,
> Amidst the youths, their vigour in the race
> Or feats of wrestling, while their airy robe
> Flies back, and leaves their limbs uncover'd.

The skirts of the habit which the virgins wore were not sewed to the bottom, but opened at the sides as they walked, and discovered the thigh (*see* plate 19, figs. 7 and 8). Sophocles very plainly writes:—

> "Still in the light dress struts the vain Hermionè,
> Whose opening folds display the naked thigh."

In the Spartan marriages the bridegroom carried off the bride by violence; and she was never chosen in a tender age, but when she had arrived at full maturity. Then the woman who had the direction of the wedding cut the bride's hair close to the skin, dressed her in man's clothes, laid her on a mattress, and left her in the dark. Marriage was strongly insisted upon by the Spartan lawgiver, and even as late as the days of Lysander bachelors and widowers who shunned re-entering the marriage state, were obliged to march in an ignominious procession singing songs against themselves. They were besides excluded from the exercises where the young virgins contended naked; and once a year they were personally chastised by the women, who were rendered by their gymnastic exercises uncommonly muscular and well developed. In one of the plays of Aristophanes, a Spartan lady is thus complimented by her friend Lysistratè,— "My beloved Lampito, how handsome you are; your complexion is so fine, and your person so full and healthy; why, you could strangle a bull." "Yes," replies Lampito, "I fancy I could, for I exercise myself in jumping till my heels touch my back." Doubtless such personal vigour was not rare at Lacedæmon; and the anticipation and reception of an annual chastisement from such bouncing dames would do a good deal to disturb the peaceful repose of single blessedness, and lead the perplexed bachelor to avoid the ills he knew, and fly to others that he knew not of.

The precautions of Lycurgus against weakness, effeminacy, and luxury extending to dress, the young women wore only a woollen robe, loose at one side, and fastened by clasps over the shoulder. Embroidery, gold, and precious stones were thought too despicable for the adornment of noble and respectable women, but were only used by courtesans, in the best period of the Spartan fame. Later, however, when Sparta gained immense quantities of gold and silver after the Peloponnesian war, and the laws of Lycurgus were neglected, the Spartans showed themselves as weakly fond of luxury as their neighbours. The women, too, lost much of their noble simplicity, and with it the serene womanly modesty for which they had been distinguished. They made such evil use of the freedom which the laws of Lycurgus had given them, that they got a bad name on account of their wantonness and excessive desire for pleasure. They are stigmatized by Euripides with the epithet of ἀνδρομανεῖς, that is, *possessed with furious love of*, and, as it were, *running mad after men*.

Fig. 5. Dorian Costume.

Scanty costume was regarded as a sign of hardiness. The Lydians were originally a hardy and warlike people, who wore scanty costume. When they revolted, Crœsus advised Cyrus to pardon them, "and enjoin them to keep no weapons of war in their possession; and enjoin them to wear tunics under their cloaks, and buskins on their feet; and require them to teach their sons to play on the cithara, to strike the guitar, and to sell by retail; and then you will see them becoming women instead of men, so that they will never give you any apprehensions about their revolting." Afterwards the Lydians became effeminate, wore long dresses, and were called the tunic-trailing Lydians.

Herodotus says (v. 87, 88) that the whole ancient Grecian dress was a woollen dress similar to that which was called Dorian or Spartan. The reason of the change was that in a fight between the Æginetæ and Argives on the one side, and the Athenians on the other, the Attic or Athenian army was all destroyed except one man. "On his return to Athens he gave an account of the disaster, and the wives of the men who had gone on the expedition against Ægina, when they heard it, being enraged that he alone of the whole number should be saved, crowded round this man, and piercing him with the clasps of their garments, each asked him where her own husband was? Thus he died. This action of the women seemed to the Athenians more dreadful than the disaster itself; however, as they had no other way of punishing the women, they compelled them to change their Doric costume for the Ionian. For before that time the wives of the Athenians wore the Dorian dress, which nearly resembles the Corinthian; they changed it, therefore, for a linen tunic, that they might not use clasps.

Yet if we follow the truth, this garment is not originally Ionian but Carian, for the whole ancient Grecian dress of the women was the same as that which we now call Dorian. In consequence of this event, it became customary with both the Argives and the Æginetæ to do this: to make their clasps one-half larger than the measure before established, and that the women should chiefly dedicate clasps in the temple of these deities; and

Fig. 6. Lycian Dresses from the Xanthus Sculptures.
(Probably the same as the Carian Dress.)

to bring no other Attic article within the temple, not even a pitcher; but a law was made that they should drink there in future from vessels of their own country. Accordingly, from that time the wives of the Argives and Æginetæ, on account of their quarrel with the Athenians, continued even to my time to wear clasps larger than formerly."

Owing to the warmth of the climate, and the good

SIMPLICITY OF ANCIENT GREEK COSTUME.

taste of the Greeks, superfluous or tight articles of dress were not used. Though more fully clad in most parts of Greece than in Sparta, the costume of the young girls and women was such as allowed the body to develope its natural beauty, and permitted a graceful freedom of motion.

Simplicity of attire was in Greece, as elsewhere, the mark of the age of refinement. In the earlier times the dresses of both men and women seem to have depended for their effect on their rich embroidery; whereas in the age of Phidias, and later times, the dress of the women especially, depends for its beauty on the softness of the material, the graceful hanging or flow of its lines, and the way in which it drapes, but does not conceal, the form beneath it.

In most early work a stiffness of line may be observed, which may be in part due to the want of skill in the sculptor or draughtsman, but which is probably more due to the hardness and stiffness of the material of which the dresses were made. In some early works, however, the women wear a jacket or jersey which clings close to the figure, and this jacket is seamed by the sculptor into minute lines, which resemble in effect the lines in knitted worsted work (see plate 104).

As the Greek ladies thirty centuries ago were accomplished in the more difficult arts of spinning, weaving, embroidery, and all kinds of needlework, it is not likely that the art of knitting, which is the art which female children learn most easily, would be unknown to them.

The two chief kinds of garments in use were the ἐνδύματα (endymata), which were put on next the naked body like a shirt, and the ἐπιβλήματα (epiblēmata) or περιβλήματα (periblēmata), which might either be used over the shirt as a cloak, or by itself alone as the sole covering of the body. These two parts of dress might be infinitely varied in arrangement, but their essential form remained pretty much the same in the middle and later periods.

The chief form of the end. ., which originally only signified raiment or dress, was the χιτών (chitōn), a form of which was used both by men and women—the women's chiton being long and reaching to the feet, the men's short and scarcely reaching to the knees. Chitōnion and chitōniskos were the names for little chitons; no undershirt seems to have been used. The expressions μονοχίτων (monochitōn) and ἀχίτων (achitōn) only indicate that in the first case the chiton alone was worn, and in the other that the ἱμάτιον (himation) or cloak was worn without the chiton. The chiton was subjected to many little refinements in process of time, though its leading features remained nearly the same. It was a long piece of cloth arranged round the body so that the arm could be put through a hole in the closed side, the two ends of the open side being fastened over the opposite shoulder by means of a button or clasp; on this latter side the chiton was in some cases stitched, in some completely open (plate 19); sometimes it was open from the thigh downwards, and the two sides could be linked together by means of studs or buttons. In other examples the chiton had short sleeves, and resembled pretty much the chemises worn by women at the present day. Sometimes the sleeves were continued down to the elbow, but instead

THE CHITON.

of being stitched at the seam, the two sides were linked together by studs, which allowed the naked flesh to peep through at intervals (see plates 1, 3, 4); other examples have the sleeve down to the wrist (see fig. 18). Round the waist or at the hips, or at both places, the chiton was held to the body by a ribbon or girdle; when it was desired to tuck up the dress, it was shortened by being pulled through the girdle. The goddess Diana (Artemis) is frequently shown with her chiton tucked up, so that she might follow the chase with greater freedom. Plates 58 and 59 represent her with the chiton in its normal state; plates 55, 56, 57 show the shortened chiton.

Fig. 7.

The Spartan women wore the Dorian chiton, which was short-skirted and simply made. It had a slit at both sides for the arms, and was fastened by clasps or buttons over both shoulders (see fig. 7); it was also made like the ἐξωμίς (exōmis), used by workmen, fishermen, and sailors, whose occupations required that the right arm should not be encumbered—in this it was fastened over the left shoulder (fig. 5).

The earlier form of the long chiton (χιτών ποδήρης), which gives the effect of a bib hanging over the breast, may be best understood by taking two pieces of cloth, each about one-half longer than the height of the body to the shoulders; let three-fourths of the superfluous half fall over in front, place the one piece at the back, and the

Fig. 8.

Fig. 9. Caryatide, from the Erechtheion.

other at the front of the figure, and pin or clasp them through the folded edges together at the shoulder. The pin should be passed through the cloth some distance from the outside edge, so as to let the angle pieces go into folds. The superfluous parts will hang outside, over the bosom in the one case, and down the back in the other. The sides are now quite open; they may be left thus, they may be joined together at intervals by studs or buttons, or one or both sides may be stitched together as far as the armpits. All these modes have their representatives in Greek art (see plate 9, fig. 8). The bottom edge will trail on the ground; but when the under part of the chiton is pulled up through the girdle (ζώνιον στρόφιον), enough to leave the toes visible, the fulness thus gained is allowed to pass over and conceal the zone. The artistic and simple effect of the draping in the Caryatides of the Erechtheion is produced by a single garment arranged as described. The κόλπος (kolpos) was the name applied to the picturesque folds which were formed by the hanging corners of the loose edge of the chiton. These could be varied considerably by merely shifting the position of the pin or button that held them at the shoulder, or by putting on a series of buttons. Perhaps the names διπλοΐς, δίπλαξ, or διπλοΐδιον (diplois, diplax, or diploidion), which signify a garment doubled, may have been given at one time to the folded or hanging part of the chiton, but it was afterwards applied to the himation or cloak when worn double folded (see plates 39 and 63).

In the age of Pericles no sleeves seem to be attached to the chiton; and in the "Banquet of Xenophon," Carmides twits Socrates with taking delight in placing his shoulder accidentally against the naked shoulder of a beautiful young lady, who was presumably dressed in the fashionable costume of Athens in the time of Pericles. He says:—"Nevertheless, I remember very well, and I believe you do so too, Socrates, that being one day in company with Critobulus's beautiful sister, who resembles him so much, as we were searching for a passage in some author, you held your head very close to that beautiful virgin; and I thought you seemed to take pleasure in touching her naked shoulder with yours." "Good God!" replied Socrates. "I will tell you truly how I was punished for it for five days after; I thought I felt in my shoulder a certain tickling pain, as if I had been bit by gnats or pricked with nettles; and I must confess, too, that during all that time I felt a certain hitherto unknown pain at my heart."

The chief alterations of varying fashion applied to the arrangement of the diploïdion, which reached either to the part under the bosom, or was prolonged as far as the hips; its front and back parts might either be clasped together across the shoulders, or the two rims or edges might be pulled across the upper arm as far as the elbow, and fastened in several places by means of buttons or agraffes, so that the naked arm became visible in the intervals, by means of which the sleeveless chiton received the appearance of one with sleeves. Where the diploïdion was detached from the chiton, it formed a kind of hand-

Fig. 10.

some cape; which, however, in its shape strictly resembled the diploïdion proper. This cape was most

VARIETIES OF THE DIPLOÏDION.

likely called by the Greeks ἀμπέχονιον. Its shape was considerably modified by fashion, taking sometimes the form of a close-fitting jacket (fig. 10), at others (when the sides remained open) that of a kind of shawl, the ends of which sometimes equalled in length the chiton itself (plates 1, 5, 6, figs. 11, 22). In the latter case the ampechonion was naturally three times as long as it was wide. In antique pictures women sometimes wear a shorter chiton over the χιτὼν ποδήρης. A great many varieties of dress are distinguishable in the vase paintings. These, as a rule, represent realistic scenes and actual dresses as worn by the Greek ladies; whereas the sculptures of the Phidian and later periods very often represent an ideal type in no way authorized by the earlier Greek literature.

Fig. 11.

The ἐνδύματα (endymata), or garments worn next the skin, or completing an indoor costume, were supplemented by the περιβλήματα (periblémata), to which order cloaks and outside wraps belong. Some of these resembled the Roman togas, but they were worn in Greece in a freer and more varied manner than was customary in Rome. The ἱμάτιον (himation) was arranged so that the one corner was thrown over the left shoulder in front, so as to be attached to the body by means of the left arm.

On the back, the dress was pulled towards the right side, so as to cover it completely up to the right shoulder, or at least to the armpit, in which latter case the right shoulder remained uncovered. Finally, the himation was again thrown over the left shoulder, so that the ends fell over the back (see plates 23 to 49). A second way of arranging the himation which left the right arm free was found to be picturesque, and was therefore much used in pictures and statues. The Parthenon sculptures, representing the maidens carrying hydrai, may be considered the common type. In order to preserve the folds, and prevent the dress from slipping from the shoulders, the Greeks used to sew small weights into the corners.

General Description of Greek Female Costume.

The general description given by Mr. Hope, author of "The Costumes of the Ancients," is as follows :—

"With regard to the attire of the body, the innermost article, that garment which does not indeed appear always to have been worn, but which, whenever worn, was always next the skin, seems to have been of a light creasy stuff, similar to the gauzes of which to this day the eastern nations make their shirts. The peculiar texture of this stuff not admitting of broad folds or drapery, this under garment was in early times cut into shapes fitting the body and arms very closely, and confined or joined round the neck, and down the sleeves, by substantial hems or stays of some stouter tissue. But even this part of the attire seems in later times to have been worn very wide and loose round the body, and often at the shoulders; where, as in the figures of Minerva and of the bearded Bacchus, the sleeves are gathered up in such a way as totally to lose their shape.

"The outer garment assumes in the figures of the old style an infinite variety of shapes, but seems always to have been studiously plaited, so as to form a number of flat and parallel folds across its surface, a zigzag line along its edge, and a sharp point at each of its angles.

"Though the costume of the Greeks seems to have been more particularly of the sort just described at the periods when the sieges of Troy and of Thebes were supposed to have taken place, and is in fact represented as such in the more ancient monuments relative to those events, the later works of art, nevertheless, even where they profess to represent personages belonging to those early ages, usually array them in the more unconfined habiliments of more recent times. In the male figures even of such primeval heroes as a Hercules, an Achilles, and a Theseus, we generally find the long formal ringlets of the heroic ages omitted for the short crops of the historic periods.

"I shall now enter into a somewhat greater detail with regard to the different pieces of which was composed the Grecian attire.

"The principal vestment both of men and of women, that which was worn next the skin, and which consequently, whenever more than one different garment was worn over the other, was undermost, bore in Greek the name of χιτών, in Latin that of *tunica*. It was of a light tissue; in earliest times made of wool, in later periods of flax, and last of all, of flax mixed with silk, or even pure silk. Its body was in general composed of two square pieces sewed together on the sides. Sometimes it remained sleeveless, only offered openings for the bare arms to pass through, and was confined over the shoulders by means of clasps or buttons; at other times it had very long and wide sleeves; and these were not unfrequently, as in the figures of Minerva and the bearded Bacchus, gathered up under the armpits, so as still to leave the arms in a great measure bare. Most usually, however, the body of the tunic branched out into a pair of tight sleeves, reaching to near the elbow, which in the most ancient dresses were close, with a broad stiff band running down the seams, and in more modern habiliments open in their whole length, and only confined by means of small buttons carried down the arms, and placed so near the edge of the stuff as in their interval to show the skin. In very richly embroidered tunics the sleeves sometimes descended to the wrists, in others they hardly reached halfway down the upper arm.

Fig. 12.

Fig. 13.

"The tunic was worn by females

either quite loose or confined by a girdle; and this girdle was either drawn tight round the waist, or loosely slung round the loins. Often when the tunic was very long, and would otherwise have entangled the feet, it was drawn over the girdle in such a way as to conceal the latter entirely underneath its folds. It is not uncommon to see two girdles of different widths worn together, the one very high up, and the other very low down, so as to form between the two in the tunic a puckered interval; but this fashion was only applied to short tunics by Diana, by the wood nymphs, and by other females fond of the chase, the foot-race, and such other martial exercises as were incompatible with long petticoats.

Fig. 11.

Fig. 14.

"Over this tunic or under-garment, which was made to reach the whole length of the body down to the feet, Grecian females generally, though not always, wore a second and more external garment, only intended to afford an additional covering or protection to the upper half of the person. This species of bib seems to have been composed of a square piece of stuff, in form like our shawls or scarfs, folded double, so as to be apparently reduced to half its original width; and was worn with the doubled part upwards, and the edge or border downwards next the zono or girdle. It was suspended round the chest and back in such a way that its centre came under the left arm, and its two ends hung down loose under the right arm; and according as the piece was square or oblong, these ends either only reached to the hips or descended to the ankles. The whole was secured by means of two clasps or buttons, which fastened together the fore and hind part over each shoulder.

Fig. 16.

"In later times this bib, from a square piece of stuff doubled, seems to have become a mere single narrow slip, only hanging down a very short way over the breasts, and allowing the girdle, even when fixed as high as possible, to appear underneath.

"The peplum constituted the outermost covering of the body. Among the Greeks it was worn in common by both sexes, but was chiefly reserved for occasions of ceremony or of public appearance, and as well in its texture as in its shape, seemed to answer to our shawl. When very long and ample, so as to admit of being wound twice round the body—first under the arms, and the second time over the shoulders—it assumed the name of diplax. In rainy or cold weather it was drawn over the head. At other times this peculiar mode of wearing it was expressive of humility or of grief, and was adopted by men and women when in mourning, or when performing sacred rites; on both which accounts it was thus worn by Agamemnon when going to sacrifice his daughter.

"This peplum was never fastened on by means of clasps or buttons, but only prevented from slipping off through the intricacy of its own involutions. Endless were the combinations which these exhibited; and in nothing do we see more ingenuity exerted, or more fancy displayed, than in the various modes of making the peplum form grand and contrasted draperies. Indeed, the different degrees of simplicity or of grace observable in the throw of the peplum were regarded as indicating the different degrees of rusticity or of refinement inherent in the disposition of the wearer.

For the sake of dignity, all the goddesses of the highest class, Venus excepted, wore the peplum; but for the sake of convenience, Diana generally had hers furled up and drawn tight over the shoulders and round the waist, so as to form a girdle, with the ends hanging down before or behind. Among the Greeks the peplum never had, as among the barbarians, its whole circumference adorned by a separate fringe, but only its corners loaded with little metal weights or drops, in order to make them hang down more straight and even.

"A veil of lighter tissue than the peplum was often

worn by females. It served both as an appendage of rank and as a sign of modesty. On the first account it is seen covering the diadem of Juno, the mitra of Ceres, and the turreted crown of Cybele, and of the emblematical figures of cities and of provinces; and on the latter account it is made, in ancient representations of nuptials, to conceal the face of the bride. Penelope, when urged to state whether she preferred staying with her father or following her husband, is represented expressing her preference of the latter by merely drawing her veil over her blushing features.

"Greatly diversified were, among the Grecian females, the coverings of both extremities. Ladies reckoned among the ornaments of the head the mitra or bushel-shaped crown, peculiarly affected by Ceres; the tiara or crescent-formed diadem, worn by Juno and by Venus; and ribands, rows of beads, wreaths of flowers, nettings, fillets, skewers, and gewgaws innumerable. The feet were sometimes left entirely bare. Sometimes they were only protected underneath by a simple sole, tied by means of thongs or strings, disposed in a variety of elegant ways across the instep and round the ankle; and sometimes they were also shielded above by means of shoes or half-boots, laced before, and lined with the fur of animals of the feline tribe, whose muzzle and claws were disposed in front. Earrings in various shapes, necklaces in numerous rows, bracelets in the form of hoops or snakes for the upper and lower arms, and various other trinkets were in great request, and were kept in a species of casket or box called pyxis, from the name of the wood of which it was originally made; and these caskets, as well as the small oval hand-mirrors of metal (the indispensable insignia of the courtesan), the umbrella, the fan formed of leaves or of feathers, the calathus or basket of reeds to hold the work, and all the other utensils and appendages intended to receive, to protect, or to set off whatever appertained to female dress and embellishment, are often represented on the Grecian fictile vases."

Usual Colours and Materials of Robes.

White and gold seem in early times to have formed a favourite arrangement of colour for feminine dress, as may be seen from the description of Nausicaa in the fifth book of the Odyssey:—

"The nymph's fair head a veil transparent graced;
Her swelling loins a radiant zone embraced
With flowers of gold: an under robe, unbound,
In snowy waves flow'd glittering on the ground."

The fashion was continued in the peplos of Athéné, which was renewed every four years by the maidens of Athens, who worked the garment under the superintendence of two of the select noble virgins who had taken part in the Arrephoria or Ersephoria, a festival in honour of Athéné and Ersa, a daughter of Cecrops. The noble virgins who took the leading part in this festival were also dressed in white apparel, set off with ornaments and embroidery of gold. The white dresses belonging to the ladies of the household of King Alcinoüs are referred to as follows:—

"Then emulous the royal robes they lave,
And plunge the vestures in the cleansing wave
(The vestures cleansed, o'erspread the shelly sand;
Their snowy lustre whitens all the strand)."—*Od.* vi.

When about to supplicate the gods for the return of Odysseus, Penelope prepares thus :—

"She bathed: and, robed in white, with all her train."

At the Thesmophoria, a festival in honour of Ceres (Δημήτηρ, Déméter, in the Greek), the women who officiated were clad in white apparel, to intimate their spotless innocence. In various parts of Homer the dazzling whiteness of the dress of ladies is referred to. Other colours were also in use.

Hesiod speaks of "Enyo of saffron vestment;" and at the Brauronia, a festival of Diana, the most remarkable persons in the solemnity were young virgins wearing yellow gowns, who were consecrated to Diana.

In Lysistrata, Calonice asks: "What prudent or brilliant action could women accomplish? We, who sit decked out, wearing saffron-coloured robes, and beautified, and wearing loose Cimmerian vests and sandals?" Lysistrata replies: "For in truth these are even the very things which I expect will save us; the little saffron-coloured robes, and the unguents, and the sandals, and the alkanet root, and the transparent vests." Calonice says: "Then by the two goddesses, I'll get me a saffron robe dyed." Wheelwright's version of the first part of the passage is :—

"Who sit dress'd out with flowers and blazing robes
Of saffron hue and richly broider'd o'er,
With loose Cimmerian vests and circling sandals."

Saffron seems to have been the fashionable colour for ladies in Athens in the time of Aristophanes. Saffron-coloured robes are constantly referred to in his comedies.

SAFFRON-COLOURED ROBES.

Besides many hints in Lysistrata about the overwhelming effect of the colour in fascinating the men, such as—
"Wearing a saffron-coloured robe, and decked out, so that my husband may be as much as possible enamoured," we have a scene in the Thesmophoriazusæ in which Mnesilochus, the father-in-law of Euripides, disguises himself as a woman, in order to plead for the tragic poet at the Thesmophoria, thus :—

"*Agath.* What? First take and put on a saffron-coloured robe.
Mnes. (*sniffing at it*). By Venus, it smells sweetly. . . . Now bring me a girdle.
Eur. There. . . . We want a head-dress and head-band.
Agath. Nay, rather, see here's a woman's cap to put round him, which I wear by night.
Eur. By Jove, but it's even very suitable.
Mnes. Will it fit me? (*Puts it on.*)
Agath. By Jove, but it's capital.
Eur. Bring an upper garment! (ἐγκύκλον).
Agath. Take it from the little couch.
Eur. We want shoes.
Agath. Here, take mine. . . ."

"This funny toilet scene," says Droysen, "is especially worthy of notice, on the account that it teaches that we are not to imagine the dress of the Athenian women to have been by any means so simple as it is represented in ancient sculptures."

The Agamemnon of Æschylus, in the chorus referring to Iphigenia, says :—

"And pouring to the ground her garments of saffron dye."

Aristophanes makes Lysistrata say :—

"As soon as I was seven years of age I carried the peplus; and then when I was ten I was a meal-grinder to Diana; and then I was

Arctos at the Brauronia, *wearing the saffron-coloured robe;* and at length, when I was a beautiful girl, I carried the basket, wearing a chain of figs."—*Lysistrata.*

In the Ecclesiazusæ of Aristophanes the old woman says: "For I am standing idle, painted over with white lead, and clad in *a saffron-coloured robe,* and humming a tune to myself."

In another place Blepyrus, in reply to a neighbour who asks why he is dressed in yellow, says: "I have come out with my wife's *little saffron-coloured robe.*" The wives had taken away the men's garments, had stolen into the public assembly, and had thus obtained a majority of votes.

In another part of the same play the young man calls an old woman an "Empusa clothed in a bloody blister," alluding to the flame-coloured κροκωτόν which she had on.

Plautus gives a formidable list of artizans who contributed to the complete adornment of a Greek lady of fashion; but as he was a Latin writer, he grafted many Roman customs on the Greek characters of his plays. He was, moreover, the product of a later time, when artifice had a larger share in the production of beauty than in the times of Homer, Hesiod, Æschylus, and others quoted in this book. Plautus died 184 years before the Christian era. His list, taken from Aulularia, is as follows:—"There stands the scourer, the embroiderer, the goldsmith, the woollen manufacturer, retail dealers in figured skirts, dealers in women's underclothing, dyers in flame colour, dyers in violet, dyers in wax colour, or else sleeve-makers or perfumers; wholesale linendrapers, shoe-makers, squatting cobblers, slipper-makers; sandal-

makers stand there; stainers in mallow colour stand
there; hair-dressers make their demands, botchers their
demands; bodice-makers stand there; makers of kirtles
take their stand. Now you would think them got rid of.
These make way, others make their demands; 300 duns
are standing in your hall; weavers, lace-makers, casket-
makers, are introduced; the money's paid them. You
would think you had got rid of them by this, when dyers
in saffron colours come sneaking along; or else there's
always some horrid plague or other which is demanding
something."

The Romans adopted the fashions of Greece; they
translated and adapted Greek plays, and used extensively
Greek quotations in ordinary speech.

Though modified considerably to suit a Roman audience,
we may assume that the translations from, or the adapta-
tions of Greek plays executed by Plautus represent with
tolerable fidelity the Greek manners of his time. After
the simplicity of the best period of Greek costume, a
habit of extravagance in female dress seems to have set
in. Plautus makes Epidicus say:—

"What's there wonderful in that? As though many women didn't
go through the streets decked out with farms upon them. ... Why,
what new names every year these women are finding for their clothing
—the thin tunic, the thick tunic, frilled linen-cloth, chemises, bor-
dered shifts, the marigold or saffron-coloured dress, the under-petti-
coat or else the light vermilion dress, the hood, the royal or foreign
robe, the wave pattern, or the feather pattern, the wax or the apple
tint."

Generally speaking, in the heroic and Homeric periods
the colours and adornments were richer and more varied
than in later and more refined times. In early times the

quality and rarity of the cloth, the expense of the dye used, and the richness of the embroidery, were the things that distinguished the dresses of noble ladies from those of meaner rank; but when refinement had made some progress,* and richness of apparel no longer meant that the wearer was distinguished, powerful, or a leader of fashion, the cut of the garments, the mode of wearing the chiton and himation, and subtle distinctions dictated

* The change is very marked between the taste in dress in the time of Homer and that of Euripides. In the first, the great men and women wear, as a rule, garments enriched with gold embroidery, as in the description of the dress of Odysseus in Od. xix. In Euripides we find this stigmatized as barbarian finery.

In the Iphigenia we read :—

"And he who, according to the story told by men, once judged the goddesses, coming from Phrygia to Lacedæmon, flowered in the vesture of his garments, and glittering with gold, barbarian finery, loving Helen, who loved him, he stole and bore her away."

Æschylus, on the other hand, being a more faithful antiquarian, preserves the Homeric richness in the style of dress of his characters; as in the Choephori, when, after the slaughter of Ægisthus, Orestes speaks of the stain of the blood damaging the various hues of the embroidery, and in another part of the same play says: "Behold this web, the work of thy hand and the strokes of the shuttle, and on it the delineation of wild beasts."

In Agamemnon he makes his hero say to Clytemnestra: "Pamper me not after the fashions of women, nor as though I were a barbaric monarch, gape-out to me an outcry of earth-prostrate homage, nor make my path obnoxious to the evil eye by strewing it with vestments. With these, indeed, it is fitting to honour the gods; but for one who is mortal *to walk on embroidered purple* is for me by no means free from dread; I bid thee reverence me as a man, not as a god. *Without carpetings and gay fineries my fame speaks clearly forth;* and to be free from evil thoughts is God's best gift." (The inventor of Peace with Honour was probably not aware of this passage when he trod on the red cloth on his return from Berlin.)

by what we now call good taste, were the points at which the Greek ladies chiefly aimed. The rich gold embroideries, crowned with representations of gods, men, and animals, gave place first to "simpler embroidery of flowers" (*see* dress of Aphroditè, page 56), and by degrees even this decoration was confined to the borders of the garments, and was not spread all over the surface of the dress, as had previously been the custom. Modest women confined themselves to plain garments, of which the usual colour was white. (Courtesans were obliged, by one of Solon's laws, to wear flowered garments, in order to distinguish them from the respectable women.) But though we may take this as a general rule, it was by no means invariable. A passion for saffron or flame-coloured garments would break out occasionally, just as a taste for mauve, cardinal red, or æsthetic tones takes place in the present century; but as the wearers of these colours, though prominent and attracting attention, are a small minority compared with the bulk of their countrywomen who adhere to the sober colours usually adopted by English ladies, so we may take it that the saffron-coloured robe-wearing Athenians whom Aristophanes holds up to ridicule were not more numerous comparatively than the æsthetic maidens whom Gilbert and "Punch" have forced into notoriety. The fanciful colours would have their day among the frivols of Athens, and then vanish; while the pure tints * with which

* "Then also, in truth to Olympus, from earth with-its-broad-ways shall Shame and Retribution, having abandoned men, depart, *when they have clad their fair skin in white raiment*, to the tribe of the immortals. . . ."—*Hesiod.*

refinement and chastity had been associated by all the poets would throughout all time continue to be the apparel of the virgins and the noble matrons who trode proudly in golden sandals at the Panathenæa, and the other festivals in which the nobly born took part.

The Romans, as well as the Greeks and Jews, seem to have used chalk and pipe-clay to renew the whiteness of their garments. This habit is noticed in the Aululuria. The epithet of "whited sepulchres" applied to the Pharisees would be the more stinging when these men were wearing garments, the uncleanness of which was concealed by a coating of chalk.

Purple is often referred to in Homer, and though usually distinctive of kingly or military rank, and used by men, instances occur in Homer's works of its being worn by ladies, as in the following line:—

"Her purple garment veil'd the falling tear."—*Od.* iv.

For carpets and bed-clothes it seems to have been extensively used in the heroic period:—

"A purple carpet spread the pavement wide."

"With purple robes inwrought, and stiff with gold."—*Od.* vi.

". . . They spread
The downy fleece to form the slumbrous bed,
And o'er soft palls of purple grain, unfold
Rich tapestry, stiff with inwoven gold."—*Od.* iv.

Its use for ladies' garments is thus referred to by Euripides:—"There is a rock near the ocean distilling water, which sends forth from its precipices a flowing fountain, wherein they dip their urns; where was a friend of mine wetting the purple vests in dew of the stream, and she laid them down on the back of the warm, sunny cliff: from hence first came to me the report concerning my mistress, that she, worn with the bed of sickness, keeps her person within the house, and that fine vests voil her auburn head."—Hippolytus.

Variegated colours were also used for robes, as may be seen from the extracts already quoted; gold also formed usually an important part of the decoration:—

> " The largest mantle her rich wardrobes hold,
> Most prized for art, and labour'd o'er with gold "—(*Il.* vi.),

is to be offered up to the goddess by the Trojans.

Woven gold work is also referred to in the following passage:—"After this, they said, that this king descended alive into the place which the Greeks call Hades, and there played at dice with Ceres, and sometimes won, and other times lost, and that he came up again and brought with him as a present from her a napkin of gold." —Herodotus, ii. 122.

Wool was used principally by the Dorians, and linen by the Ionians, but a chiton of linen and a himation of wool were not uncommon.

Homer refers to—

> " The maids in soft cymars of linen dress'd."—*Il.* xviii.

For women's dresses, besides wool and linen, byssos, probably a kind of cotton, was used. The material of the celebrated dresses woven in the isle of Amorgos, which were similar to our fine muslin and cambrics, consisted of a very fine kind of flax. Silk was known in

Fig. 17.

Asia at a very early period, but it was not introduced into Greece till a later date. Sometimes the woven silk was brought, at others silk in its raw state, which was spun into fine transparent silk gauze, more than equal in transparency to the amorgina, or cambric of Amorgos. These diaphanous dresses, when clinging closely to the skin, allowed the colour of flesh and veins to be seen through them.

In one important matter Greek ladies differed from modern ladies of all nations. Black was never used by the Greeks as ordinary dress, but solely as the mark of grief and mourning. It was the colour of death and the raiment of the Furies. To go in a black dress to an entertainment would be regarded among the Greeks as ominous of misfortune and sorrow. The Romans followed the Greeks in this as in many others of their customs; and Cicero asks, "What person was ever found to sup in black." The tragedies of Æschylus and Euripides are draped in black.

"Will any means of grace appear? or must I cut my locks, and clothe me even now in black array of garments?"

asks the Semichorus in Alcestis.

"Neither do thou clothe them in black garments,"

says Iphigenia, meaning that her sisters should not mourn for her.

"I will exchange my white garments for black."

says Helen when she is told (falsely) that Menelaus has perished. (Helen, Eurip.) And in the same play Theoclymenus asks her:—

"Why hast thou put black garments on thy form in exchange for white?"

In the chorus of Furies in Æschylus' play of that name, we read:—

"Of white garments am I ever destitute and devoid. For I take upon myself the overthrow of houses when Ares (Mars), being kindred, has slain a friend. . . . At our approach clad in our black garments, and at the hated dances of our feet."

In the Choëphori, Orestes cries out at the oncoming Furies:—

"Ah, ah, ye handmaids, here they are in the guise of Gorgons in sable vestments, and entwined with densely woven snakes."

Mourners usually dressed in black, and muffled up their heads when they went abroad, as:—

"Her face, wrapped in a veil, declared her woes"

(see plates 26 and 27). Orestes, persuading Electra to leave off mourning, bids her unveil:—

"Pull off your veil, dear sister, and forbear
This grief. . . ."

Nor was this the fashion for women only, for Adrastus came to Theseus after his loss at Thebes, κατήρης χλανιδίοις; wherefore Theseus speaks thus to him:—

"Speak out, unfold your head, refrain from tears."

Admetus, on the death of Alcestes, says:—

"But now the groan instead of hymeneals, and black array instead of white robes, usher me into my deserted couch."—*Alcestes.*

Veils.

The veil was of lighter material than the peplum, and was worn by females of rank and as a sign of modesty. "Penelope, when urged to state whether she preferred to stay with her father or to follow her husband, is represented as expressing her preference of the latter by drawing her veil over her blushing features." Afterwards, when she comes into the hall, where the suitors are, we read that—

"A veil of richest texture wrought she wears;"

and again,—

"A veil translucent, o'er her brow display'd."
Odyssey, xviii.

Leucothea gives her veil, or scarf, to Odysseus. In the Hymn to Aphroditè it is said :—

" For for a veil she shined in an attire
That cast a radiance past the ray of fire."

Of Nausicaa we learn that—

"The nymph's fair head a veil transparent graced."

It is evident that the veil was thin enough to be seen through. This also appears from these words of Iphigenia :—

" But o'er mine eyes the veil's fine texture spread;
This brother in my hands, who now is lost,
I saw but clasp'd not."
Euripides, Iphigenia in Tauris, 373.

When the burlesque Euripides in the Thesmophoriazusæ approaches the mock Helen, he asks:—

> "Why, pray, do you sit in these sepulchral seats
> Cover'd with a veil, O female stranger?"

> "Dost thou conceal thy pendant locks with a white veil?"

asks Paul the Silentiary in the Anthology.

> "You are, O painter's brush, envious, and grudgest those who are looking on by your having concealed the golden ringlets under a head-dress."—*Anth.*

> "The lovely Heliodora offers up a veil for the face, a work partaking of the spider's web."—*Anth.*

The young Achilles, when concealed among the daughters of Lycomedes, "was wont to walk with the step of maidenhood, and to cover his hair with a veil."—Bion, xiv. Id. He was sent to Lycomedes and concealed, because his mother Thetis knew that if he went to the Trojan war he would never return.

Theocritus, in xxviii. Id., speaks of "the gauze-like garments such as women wear."

At the adornment of Pandora we read that the goddess glancing-eyed Athéné girded and arrayed "her in silver-white raiment, and from her head she held with her hands a curiously embroidered veil, a marvel to look upon."—Hesiod, "The Theogony," 572—576.

Further references to veils are to be found all through the Iliad and the Odyssey. Of Helen we read:—

> "O'er her fair face a snowy veil she threw,
> And softly sighing, from the loom withdrew."—*Il.* iii.

> "And veil'd her blushes in a silken shade."—*Il.* iii.

Aphroditè, when she appears in the battle-field, is—

"Screen'd from the foe behind her shining veil.
 . . . . .
Through her bright veil the daring weapon drove—
Th' ambrosial veil which all the Graces wore."

Of Hérè (Juno) we learn :—

"Then o'er her head she cast a veil more white
Than new-fallen snow, and dazzling as the light."—*Il.* xiv.

The veil of Athéne is richly embroidered :—

"Pallas disrobes: her radiant veil untied,
With flowers adorn'd, with art diversified."—*Il.* v.

And again in book viii. :—

"Pallas meanwhile her various veil unbound,
With flowers adorn'd, with art immortal crown'd."

When Andromache hears of Hector's death she swoons, and her veil and diadem fly far away.

The veil presented by Helen to Telemachus is thus described in the fifteenth book of the Odyssey :—

"The king selected from the glittering rows
A bowl; the prince a silver beaker chose;
The beauteous queen revolved with careful eyes
Her various textures of unnumber'd dyes,
And chose the largest; with no vulgar art
Her own fair hands embroider'd every part;
Beneath the rest it lay divinely bright,
Like radiant Hesper o'er the gems of night.
 . . . . .
The beauteous queen advancing next, display'd
The shining veil, and thus endearing said:
'Accept, dear youth, this monument of love,
Long since in better days by Helen wove;
Safe in thy mother's care the vesture lay,
To deck thy bride, and grace thy nuptial day.'"

Gold Embroidery.

In the very early times great richness was the rule for the dress of the wealthy, and as civilization increased the dresses became less ornamented. Figures and animals were in early times woven in gold into the cloth, and cloth of gold tissue was not uncommon. Schliemann discovered at Mycenæ a large number of ornamented plates of thin gold, which he thinks were at one time glued to the surface of the cloth. The young virgins who walked in the festival of the Ἀῤῥεφορία (Arrephoria) wore white apparel, set off with ornaments of gold. The peplos of the goddess Athéné, which was renewed every four years, and dedicated at the Panathenaic festival, was of a white colour, without sleeves, and embroidered with gold; upon it were described the achievements of Athéné (Minerva), especially against the giants. Zeus (Jupiter) also, and the heroes and all such as were famous for

Fig. 13. Richly Embroidered Dress.

Fig. 19.

valiant and noble exploits had their effigies in it; whence men of true courage and bravery are said to be ἄξιοι πέπλου, worthy to be portrayed in Athênê's sacred garment. The description in Homer's Odyssey of the dress of Odysseus (Ulysses) is probably no poetic fiction, but the actual description of a not unusual dress of a chief in the heroic ages; and doubtless the dress of the chieftain's wife would be equally rich :—

"A robe of military purple flow'd
  O'er all his frame; illustrious on his breast
The double-clasping gold the king confest.
In the rich woof a hound, mosaic drawn,
Bore on full stretch, and seized a dappled fawn:
Deep in the neck his fangs indent their hold;
They pant and struggle in the moving gold.
Fine as a filmy web beneath it shone
A vest, that dazzled like a cloudless sun.
The female train who round him throng'd to gaze,
In silent wonder sigh'd unwilling praise."

This ornamentation of embroidery was the work of ladies of the highest rank, as we read that in answer to Odysseus' description of the robe, Penelope says :—

"The vest much envied on your native coast,
And regal robe with figured gold emboss'd,
In happier hours my artful hand employ'd,
When my loved lord this blissful bower enjoy'd."
      Odyssey, xix. 265, 295 (Pope's Translation).

WEAVING AND EMBROIDERING.

In the Iliad, book iii., Helen is described as weaving or embroidering a veil:—

> "Her in the palace at her loom she found;
> The golden web her own sad story crown'd.
> The Trojan wars she weaved (herself the prize),
> And the dire triumph of her fatal eyes."

Pope in his note says this is a very agreeable fiction, to represent Helen weaving in a large veil the story of

Fig. 20.

the Trojan war. It is probably founded on fact, and would not be more out of the usual than the weaving or embroidering of the Conquest of England in the Bayeux tapestry, which is said to have been executed by the wife of William the Conqueror. The Greek ladies of early times were famous for their skill at the loom and with the needle. The works of Pallas, Athéné, Helen, and Penelope have already been referred to. Of the wife of Alcinoüs we read that her hours were bestowed—

> "In curious works; the whirling spindle glow'd
> With crimson threads, whilst busy damsels cull
> The snowy fleece, or twist the purpled wool."—*Od.* vi.

And again in the same book:—

> "Her royal hand a wondrous work designs;
> Around a circle of bright damsels shines,
> Part twist the threads, and part the wool dispose,
> Whilst with the purple orb the spindle glows."

Again:—

> ". . . Spread,
> The spacious loom, and mix'd the various thread,
> Where as to life the wondrous figures rise."—*Od.* ii.

Electra, when cast off by her mother after the murder of her father, says:—

"Not for splendid doings, O friends, nor for golden necklaces, am wretched I elate in mind, nor forming dances together with Argive nymphs shall I beat my foot whirled round. With tears I dance, and tears are the daily cure for wretched me. Look at my matted locks, and these rags of my garments, whether they become the royal daughter of Agamemnon and Troy, which remembers being once taken by my sire.

"*Chorus.* Great is the goddess; but come, and from me receive richly woven robes to wear, and golden additions of ornaments for thy beauty.

"*Electra.* I myself labouring mine own garments with the shuttle, or I have my body naked, and be destitute. . . . But my mother sits on a throne amid Phrygian spoils, and by her seat the Asiatic captives, whom my father took, are standing with their Idæan robes bound with golden clasps."

In the Iliad, reference is made to the embroidery of the Sidonian women of Phœnicia, whose wares were dispersed by the Phœnician trading-vessels, and by the women taking service in foreign countries. Herodotus quotes thus (ii. 116):—"Where were the variegated robes, works of the Sidonian women, which god-like Paris brought from Sidon, sailing over the wide sea, along the course by which he conveyed high-born Helen;" or to quote Pope's translation:—

"The Phrygian queen to her rich wardrobe went,
Where treasured odours breath'd a costly scent.
There lay the vestures of no vulgar art,
Sidonian maids embroider'd every part—
Whom from soft Sidon youthful Paris bore,
With Helen touching on the Tyrian shore.
Here, as the queen revolved with careful eyes
The various textures and the various dyes,
She chose a veil that shone superior far,
And glow'd effulgent as the morning star."

In a few lines preceding these, reference is made to—

"The largest mantle your full wardrobes hold,
Most prized for art and labour'd o'er with gold,
Before the goddess' honour'd knees be spread."

The Phrygians were afterwards famous for their skill in embroidery. In the time of Plautus, about 200 B.C., the Roman embroiderers were called Phrygiones (*see* Menæchmi, or the Twin Brothers, ver. 425).

At the same period Babylonian stuffs, mostly of a purple colour, richly embroidered with gold, were used as coverings for couches and other purposes (*see* Stichus, ver. 378). The Babylonians seem to have obtained fame early; in Joshua vii. 24 we read, "I saw among the spoils a goodly Babylonish garment." But according to Pliny the Elder, the people of Alexandria excelled both the Phrygians and the Babylonians in depicting in their tapestry of many threads, the figures of birds, beasts, and human beings. Alexandrian tapestry is referred to by Plautus in his Pseudolus, ver. 147, where Ballio says to the slaves, "I'll make your sides to be right thoroughly marked with thongs, so much so that not even Campanian coverlets are covered as well, nor yet Alexandrian tapestry of purple embroideries with beasts all over."

Some slaves also seem to have been accomplished in these arts, for at the funeral rites of Patroclus the first prize for the racers is :—

"A woman for the first, in beauty's bloom,
Skill'd in the needle and the labouring loom;
And a large vase, where two bright handles rise,
Of twenty measures its capacious size."—*Il.* xxiii.

Although women seem to have been well employed,

the lives of female children were not always respected. We know that among the Lacedæmonians weak children were thrown into a deep cavern in the earth, near the mountain Taygetus; and many persons exposed their children because they were unable to maintain them. Daughters especially were so treated, because they were more troublesome and expensive to educate and settle in life than sons. Posidippus cites a saying :—

"A man, though poor, will not expose his son;
But if he's rich, will scarce preserve his daughter."

Goldsmiths' Ornaments.

The discoveries by Dr. Schliemann of the golden diadems, studded scabbards, jewelled sceptres, masks, and rich embroideries, which were heaped up in the tomb of Agamemnon at Mycenæ, bear witness to the great skill of the Greek or Phœnician or Trojan jewellers who executed the work, and also prove that the superabundant reference to golden work in the Homeric poems is no poetical exaggeration, but real description of what was actually in use in the heroic and later periods. Thirty centuries ago the goldsmith's art seems to have been practised with a skill quite equal to that of the ordinary work of the present day. In many respects it decidedly displays more judgment and taste than is visible in the usual run of the manufactured gold work of the nineteenth century, and is quite equal to it in artistic manipulation.

It is not to be assumed, however, that because the golden treasures discovered by Schliemann were found at Mycenæ, they were necessarily of Greek workmanship. The inference is rather that some of these things

Fig. 21. Bracelet found at Ilios by Dr. Schliemann.

Fig. 22. Golden Diadem found at Mycenae by Dr. Schliemann. Size, 1 : 5, about.

at least were part of the Trojan spoils, gathered at the sacking of Ilion. Reference is made to these treasures in the Electra of Euripides, thus: "My mother sits on a throne amid Phrygian spoils;" and again, where Clytemnestra says, "For the houses of the gods are adorned with Phrygian spoils; but I possess in my house those chosen from the Trojan land." This view is supported by the fact that the pottery found at Mycenæ is in a much ruder style of art than is shown in the metal work; the pottery was probably indigenous, the jewellery, being most likely the workmanship of Phœnician or Phrygian artists, was brought from Ilios by the victorious Greeks. It may be further noticed that the gold work found at Ilios was trifling in quantity, whereas the pottery was exceedingly abundant: the inference naturally is that the Greeks took all the gold they could lay their hands upon, but did not trouble themselves about the Trojan crockery. As Agamemnon was the chief of the army, his share of the golden spoil would be large and splendid. For a full description, with illustrations of these early examples of the goldsmith's art, the reader is referred to "Mycenæ," and "Ilios," by Dr. Schliemann. The golden diadem and bracelet on page 51 will, however, give some idea of the style used in these works; for these illustrations we are indebted to the kindness and courtesy of Mr. John Murray, the publisher of Schliemann's beautifully illustrated volumes.

Descriptions of golden zones, baldrics, and carved and graven armour abound in Homer, but in the following extracts we have confined ourselves to references to female ornaments:—

> "An artist to my father's palace came,
> With gold and amber chains, elaborate frame;
> Each female eye the glittering links employ;
> They turn, review, and cheapen every toy."—*Od.* xv.

> "On her immortal head a crown they placed,
> Elaborate, and with all the beauties graced
> That gold could give it; of a weight so great,
> That, to impose and take it off, it had set
> Three handles on it, made for endless hold,
> Of shining brass, and all adorned with gold.
> Her soft neck all with carcanets was graced,
> That stoop'd and both her silver breasts embraced.
> *Second Hymn to Aphroditè.*

"Chains, bracelets, pendants, all their toys I wrought,"

says Hephaistos (Vulcan) to Thetis (*Il.* xviii.).

Far-beaming pendants, each gem illumined by a triple star, tremble in the ear of Hérè (see page 59).

The suitors present to Penelope earrings bright with triple stars, a bracelet rich with gold and amber, and a necklace wrought with art (see page 58).

Andromache wears a diadem. When she hears of her husband's death—

> "Her hair's fair ornaments, the braids that bound
> The net that held them, and the wreath that crown'd
> The veil and diadem, flew far away."—*Il.* xxii.

Hesiod refers to "Hébè of the golden crown," "Phœbè with golden coronet;" and in his description of the dressing of Pandora tells us that " Pallas Athéné placed around her about her head lovely garlands, fresh-budding with meadow flowers, and around her head she set a golden coronet, which renowned Hephaistos (Vulcan), lame with both feet, had made himself, having wrought it carefully by hand, out of compliment to his father Zeus. On it had been wrought many curious monsters, a marvel to view, as many as in great abundance the continent and the sea maintain. Many of these he introduced of wondrous beauty, like to living animals gifted with sounds."

Hermionè in Andromache says: "I have come hither, not indeed bearing an ornament of golden luxury around my head, nor this vesture or embroidered garments around my person." In other plays of Euripides we read:—

"The golden-decked vestment of the robe of the warlike girl."
(*Hippolita*) *Her. Fur.*

"But the daughter of Jove possesses golden mirrors, the delight of virgins.—*Eurip. Troades.*

"Celebrate Cora with her golden crown."—*Ion.*

"The children had necklaces made in the form of serpents."
Note to Ion, Eurip., Bohn.

A fine-wrought robe and a golden-turned chaplet is sent by Medea to her rival. The chorus says:—"The bride shall receive the destructive present of the golden chaplet; she wretched shall receive them, and around her golden tresses shall she place the attire of death, having received the presents in her hands. The beauty and the divine glitter of the robe will persuade her to place around her head the golden-wrought chaplet. . . . But when she saw the ornaments she refused not, but promised her husband everything; and before thy sons and their father were gone far from the house, she took and put on the variegated robes, and having placed the golden chaplet around her tresses, she arranges her hair in the radiant mirror, smiling at the lifeless image of her person. And after having risen from her seat, she goes across the chamber, elegantly tripping with snow-white feet, rejoicing greatly in the presents, looking much and oftentimes with her eye on her outstretched neck. . . . The golden chaplet indeed placed on her head was sending forth a stream of all-devouring fire, wonderful to behold, but the fine-wrought robes, the presents of thy sons, were devouring the white flesh of the hapless woman. But she having started from her seat, flies, all on fire, tossing her hair and head on this side and that side, desirous of shaking off the chaplet; but the golden wreath firmly kept its hold; but the fire, when she shook her hair, blazed out with double fury, and she sinks on the ground overcome by her sufferings."

In the Acharnians, the wife says to her daughter, as they are going to the festival:—

"Proceed, and in the crowd take especial care, that no one secretly nibbles off your golden ornaments."

The Hecuba of Euripides supplies the following:—

"Standest thou idle, thou man of most mean spirit? Hast in thy hand no robe, no ornament for the maiden?

"This I cannot; but as I can, I will, for what can I do! And collecting ornaments from among the captured women, who dwell beside me in these tents."

"What a quantity of gold she wears, like a virgin!"
Birds, Aristoph.

"Where are the myrrh-boxes of the Paphian Venus, and her upper garment all gold?"—*Anthology.*

In Callimachus's "Bath of Pallas" we read:—

"Ye maidens, ... wherefore now also bring ye only the strong oil in which Castor, in which also Heraclês anoints himself. Bring out, too, her comb all-of-gold, that she may comb her hair when she has anointed her sleek curls."

The sides of the early dresses were not stitched together, but were united from the armpits to the waist by golden clasps (see pages 16, 18, 58, 59).

In Rudens there is a description of female trinkets. In the first place there is a little sword of gold, with the name of the wearer's father inscribed; then a gold two-edged axe, inscribed with the mother's name; "next there's a little knife of silver, and two little hands linked together, and then a little bow; then there is a golden drop (bulla), which my father presented to me on my birthday."

The Dress of Aphroditè (Venus).

The attire of Aphroditè is thus minutely described in the hymn to the goddess, which has been ascribed to Homer:—

Fig. 31.

"Anchises seeing her, all his senses were
With wonder stricken; and high-taken heeds
Both of her form, brave stature, and rich weeds.
For for a veil she shined in an attire
That cast a radiance past the ray of fire.
Beneath which, wore she girt to her a gown
Wrought all with growing rose-buds, reaching down
T'her slender smalls, which buskins did divine;
Such as taught Thetis' silver feet to shine.
Her soft white neck rich carcanets embraced,
Bright, and with gold in all variety graced,

Fig. 34.

That to her breasts let down, lay there and shone
As at her joyful full the rising moon.
. . . First he took from her
The fiery weed, that was her utmost wear.
Unbuttoned next her rosy robe, and loosed
The girdle that her slender waist enclosed,
Unlaced her buskins; all her jewellery
Took from her neck and breasts, and all laid by
Upon a golden-studded chair of state."

Hymn to Aphroditè (Venus).

The "utmost" or outmost robe or veil was probably the himation, similar to those indicated in figs. 4 and 5, and plates 7 and 21 to 38. The two sides of the gown, with " growing rose-buds wrought," were joined together from the armpits to the waist by buttons or clasps, the lower portion from the waist to the feet being open at the two sides, and similar, no doubt, to that presented to Penelope by one of the suitors (*see* figs. 4 and 5, plates 15, 19, 78) :—

> " A robe Antinoüs gives of shining dyes;
> The varying hues in gay confusion rise
> Rich from the artist's hand! twelve clasps of gold
> Close to the lessening waist the vest infold;
> Down from the swelling loins the vest unbound
> Floats in bright waves redundant o'er the ground.
> A bracelet rich with gold, and amber gay,
> That shot effulgence like the solar ray,
> Eurymachus presents; and earrings bright,
> With triple stars, that cast a trembling light.
> Pisander bears a necklace wrought with art;
> And every peer, expressive of his heart,
> A gift bestows."—*Od.* xviii.

The Dress of Hérè.

Fig. 26.

In the following description of the dressing of Hérè (Juno), Homer probably only describes faithfully the toilet of a lady of rank in the early ages of Greece :—

> " Swift to her bright apartment she repairs,
> Sacred to dress, and beauty's pleasing cares:
> With skill divine had Vulcan form'd the bower
> Safe from access of each intruding power.
> Touch'd with her secret key, the doors unfold,
> Self-closed, behind her shut the valves of gold.

THE DRESS OF HÉRÈ.

Here first she bathes; and round her body pours
Soft oils of fragrance, and ambrosial showers:
The winds, perfumed, the balmy gale convey
Through heaven, through earth, and all th' aërial way:
Spirit divine! whose exhalation greets
The sense of gods with more than mortal sweets,
Thus while she breath'd of heaven, with decent pride
Her artful hands the radiant tresses tied;
Part o'er her head in shining ringlets roll'd,
Part o'er her shoulders waved like melted gold;
Around her next a heavenly mantle flow'd,
That rich with Pallas' labour'd colours glow'd:
Large clasps of gold the foldings gather'd round,
A golden zone her swelling bosom bound.
Far-beaming pendants tremble in her ear,
Each gem illumined with a triple star.
Then o'er her head she cast a veil more white
Than new-fallen snow, and dazzling as the light.
Last her fair feet celestial sandals grace.
Forth from the dome th' imperial goddess moves,
And calls the mother of the smiles and loves.

. . . With awe divine the Queen of Love
Obey'd the sister and the wife of Jove,
And from her fragrant breast the zone unbraced,
With various skill and high embroidery graced."—*Il.* xiv.

From this passage we may learn that though attendants and slaves were abundant, the Greek ladies of early times sometimes arranged their hair themselves.

Hesiod refers to Juno "as the majestic Hérè, the Argive goddess treading proudly in golden sandals."

THE DRESS OF ATHÉNÈ (MINERVA).

Pallas Athénè (Minerva) wears two distinct dresses at different times. In Olympus it is the ordinary costume of a Greek lady of high rank; but when she goes to direct the armies of the Greeks, she assumes military attire, in

Fig. 38.

which is included the ægis or shield-supporter of her father Zeus. A passage in the Iliad, book v., indicates both sorts of dress thus:—

> "Pallas disrobes; her radiant veil untied,
> With flowers adorn'd, with art diversified
> (The labour'd veil her heavenly fingers wove),
> Flows on the pavement of the court of Jove.
> Now heaven's dread arms her mighty limbs invest,
> Jove's cuirass blazes on her ample breast;
> Deck'd in sad triumph for the mournful field,
> O'er her broad shoulders hangs his horrid shield;

THE DRESS OF ATHÉNÈ.

> Dire, black, tremendous! round the margin roll'd,
> A fringe of serpents hissing guards the gold:
> Here all the terrors of grim war appear,
> Here rages Force, here tremble Flight and Fear,
> Here storm'd Contention, and here Fury frown'd;
> And the dire orb portentous Gorgon crown'd.
> The massy golden helm she next assumes,
> That dreadful nods with four o'ershading plumes."

In another place we read:—

> "Pallas meanwhile her various veil unbound,
> With flowers adorn'd, with art immortal crown'd.
> The radiant robe her sacred fingers wove
> Floats in rich waves, and spreads the court of Jove."—*Il.* viii.

> "The dreadful ægis, Jove's immortal shield,
> Blazed on her arm and lighten'd all the field;
> Round the vast orb a hundred serpents roll'd,
> Form'd the bright fringe, and seem'd to burn in gold."
>
> Pope, *Il.* ii.

Instead of serpents it would, perhaps, be more proper to read, for τῆς ἑκατὸν θύσανοι, κ.τ.λ., "From this a hundred tassels, all golden, hang waving in the air, all well twisted, and each of the value of a hundred oxen" (ἑκατόμβοιος).—See Hesiod, Shield of Heraclés, 220-230.

Fig. 17.

"The ægis, properly speaking, was the hide of the goat Amalthea, the animal that had suckled Jupiter. It was in strictness peculiar to Jove, but was worn on different occasions by both Apollo and Athénè. The skins of various quadrupeds having been used by the most ancient inhabitants of Greece for clothing and defence, we need not wonder that the goat's skin was employed in the same manner; and the particular application of it which we have now to consider will be understood from the fact that the shields of the ancient Greeks were in part supported by a belt or strap passing

Fig. 28.

over the right shoulder, and when not elevated with the shield, descending transversely to the left hip. In order that a goat's skin might serve this purpose, two of its legs would probably be tied over the right shoulder of the wearer, the other extremity being fastened to the inside of the shield. In combat, the left arm would be passed under the hide, and would raise it, together with the shield, as is shown in a marble statue of Minerva (Athéné), preserved in the museum at Naples, which, from its style of art, may be reckoned among the most ancient in existence (fig. 28. *See also* plate 66).

"Other statues of Minerva, also of great antiquity, and derived, no doubt, from some still more ancient type, represent her in a state of repose, with the goat's skin falling obliquely from its loose fastening over the right shoulder, so as to pass round the body under the left arm."—Anthon's Notes to Homer (*see* plate 70).

By a figure of speech, Homer uses the term ægis to denote not only the goat's skin, which it properly signified, but, together with it, the shield to which it belonged. By thus understanding the word, it is easy to comprehend why Athénè is said to throw her father's ægis around her shoulders (Il. v. 738; xviii. 204); and why, on one occasion, Apollo is said to hold it in his hand, and to shake it so as to terrify and confound the Greeks (Il. xv. 229, 307); and on another occasion to cover with it the dead body of Hector, in order to protect it from insult. By the later poets and artists the original conception of the ægis appears to have been forgotten or disregarded. They represent it as a breastplate covered with metal in the form of scales, not used to support the shield, but extending equally on both sides from shoulder to shoulder, as may be seen in the figure on plates 60, 61, and 67 to 73.

Herodotus says (iv. 189):—"From the Libyan women the Grecians derived the attire and ægis of Minerva's statues; for except that the dress of the Libyan women is leather, and the fringes that hang from the ægis are not serpents, but made of thongs, in all other respects they are equipped in the same way; and, moreover, the very name proves that the garb of the Palladia comes from Libya; for the Libyan women throw over their dress goats' skins without the hair, fringed and dyed with red. From these goats' skins the Grecians have borrowed the name of ægis."

When, as in the Odyssey xiii., Athénè disguises herself as a youthful swain, we are told:—

> "A graceful robe her slender body dress'd;
> Around her shoulders flew the waving vest;
> Her decent hand a shining javelin bore;
> And painted sandals on her feet she wore."

At Athens new-born infants were usually wrapped in a cloth, on which was represented the Gorgon's head, because that was inscribed on the shield of Athéné (Minerva), the protectress of the city; and thus, as it were, infants were committed to her care. Thus we read in the Ion of Euripides that when Creusa is questioned as to the appearance of the swaddling-clothes of the infant she had exposed, she replies:—

> "A Gorgon in the centre web of the garment;
> And it is fringed with serpents like the ægis—
> Two dragons glittering with golden jaws.
>
> *Ion.* For what use are these golden ornaments, tell me,
> As a necklace for a young boy to bear?"

In the same play the ægis of Athéné is described as follows:—

> "A breastplate arm'd with wreathings of a viper.
> Yes, that Athéné wears her skin upon her breast.
> *Pad.* That which they call the ægis, the accoutrement
> Of Athéné."

According to Pausanias, in the gold and ivory statue of Athéné, in the Parthenon, the goddess was represented standing, clothed in a chiton that reached to her feet. On her ægis (breastplate or shield-cover) was Medusa's head and *Victory* in ivory. She held a spear in her hand; and at her feet lay a buckler and a dragon, supposed to be Erichthonius. The Sphinx was represented on the middle of her helmet, with a griffin on each side. The statue was thirty-nine feet high, and forty talents of gold were employed on it. We learn from Plutarch that the battle with the Amazons was represented by Phidias on Athéné's shield; amongst the figures he introduced his own likeness, as a bald-headed old man taking up a great stone with both hands, and a highly finished effigy of Pericles fighting with an Amazon. The last was contrived with so much art, that the hand lifting the spear partly covered the face, and seemed to be intended to conceal the likeness, which was yet very striking. For thus introducing modern likenesses into, and as his enemies said falsifying, the historical exploits of Theseus, Phidias was thrown into prison, where he died a natural death, though some say he was taken off by poison.

Fig. 29.

THE DRESS OF BACCHANTES.

A description of Greek female costume would scarcely

be complete without some reference to the dress that was worn in the Bacchic festivals. The following extracts indicate its chief peculiarities:—

"*Œdipus.* Go then where stands the form of Bacchus unapproached on the mountains of the Mænades.

Antigone. To whom I formerly, clad in the skin of the Theban fawn, danced the sacred step of Semelè on the mountains."

Eurip. Phœnician Virgins.

"O Thebes, thou nurse of Semelè, crown thyself with ivy, flourish, flourish with the verdant yew bearing sweet fruit, and be ye crowned in honour of Bacchus with branches of oak or pine, and adorn your garments of spotted deer-skin with fleeces of white-haired sheep, and sport in holy games . . . in which Bacchus rejoices, pleased on the mountains, when after the running dance, he falls upon the plain, having a sacred garment of deer-skin . . . to twine the thyrsi, and to put on the skins of deer, and to crown the head with ivy branches."

Chorus in Eurip. Bacchæ.

Fig. 30.

"But thy mother, standing in the midst of the Bacchæ, raised a shout to wake their bodies from sleep, when she heard the lowing of the horned oxen; but they (the Bacchantes) cast off refreshing sleep from their eyes, started upright, a marvel to behold for their elegance, young, old, and virgins yet unyoked. And first they let loose their hair over their shoulders, and arranged their deer-skins, as many as had had the fastening of their knots unloosed, and they girded the dappled hides with serpents licking their jaws—and some having in their arms a kid,

ANCIENT GREEK BACCHANT COSTUME.

or the wild whelps of wolves, gave them white milk . . . . and they put on ivy chaplets and garlands of oak and blossoming yew; and one having taken a thyrsus, struck it against a rock, whence a dewy stream of water springs out; another placed her wand on the ground, and then the god sent up a spring of wine."

In the conversation between Bacchus and Pentheus we

Fig. 31.

learn, perhaps, more particularly what were the distinguishing points of the Bacchic female dress:—

"*Bac.* Put on then linen garments on your body.
Pen. What then, shall I be reckoned among women, being a man? . . .
Bac. I will spread your hair at length on your head.

Pen. What is the next point of my equipment?

Bac. A garment down to your feet; and you shall have a turban on your head.

Pen. Shall you put anything else on me besides this?

Bac. A thyrsus in your hand, and the dappled hide of a deer. . . . But this lock of hair is out of place, not as I dressed it beneath the turban.

Pen. Look, do you arrange it, for we depend on you.

Bac. And your girdle is loosened, and the fringes of your garments do not extend regularly round your legs.

Pen. They seem so to me, too, about the right foot at least; but on this side the robe sits well along the leg. . . . But shall I be more like a Bacchante holding the thyrsus in my right hand or in this?

Bac. You should hold it in your right hand, and raise it at the same time with your right foot."

The thyrsus was a spear, the head of which was struck through a pine cone.

Fig. 22.

After the Bacchante had duly honoured Bacchus in the orgies, she gave her dress as an offering to the god in the temple:—

"Porphyris of Cnidus has for thyself, Dionysus (Bacchus), placed on high before thy chapel these ornaments of her beauty and madness, namely, the chaplets on her head, and the spear with a double pine-cone, and the ankle-band, with which she acted the Bacchant freely, when after uniting to her bosom the fawn-skin decked with ivy, she frequented the orgies of Dionysus."—*Agathias.*

Favourite Colours of Hair.

The usual colour of hair among the

Greeks being dark, light-coloured hair was considered more beautiful.

The colours of hair which seem to have been most in favour with the early Greeks were golden, auburn, and red. Helen is golden, or red, or auburn haired; Hylas and Paris have the same coloured hair; Adonis has a reddish beard on his lips. Achilles has golden or ruddy hair. When disguised among the daughters of Lycomedes, he was called Pyrrha by his female companion, on account of his golden or red hair. Pyrrhus is the masculine form of the same name, and signifies fiery red, ruddy, or rosy. It is a delicate, but misleading euphemism on the part of our translators to use golden for πυρρός or πυρρόθριξ—golden-haired (χρυσόθριξ), or yellow-haired (χρυσεοκόμης) is distinct from red (πυρρός), or from reddish (πυρρώδης).

Theocritus, in Idyll ii., speaks of two of his heroes who have beards yellower than the marigold. Bacchus is thus described in the Bacchæ of Euripides:—

"And they say that some stranger has come hither, a juggler, a charmer, from the Lydian land, fragrant in hair and golden curls, florid, having in his eyes the graces of Venus, who days and nights is with them, alluring the young maidens with Bacchic mysteries; but if I catch him under this roof, I will stop him from making a noise with the thyrsus, and waving his hair, by cutting off his neck from his body."

Theocritus, in Idyll xv., says:—

"Though the beard of Adonis is red (πυρρός) all round his mouth, his kisses are soft."

In Idyll xviii. we read of the auburn-haired Menelaus;

of the golden-haired Apollo in the Suppliants of Euripides, and elsewhere.

In the literal translation of Theocritus, Id. viii., we read that both Menaclas and Daphnis were red-haired (πυρρότριχω); and in this description Polwhele finds the original of Collins's expression, "the fiery-tressed Dane." In the metrical version, however, we find "both yellow tressed and in their life's fresh spring." In Idylls vi. and xiii. the same transformations take place.

In ancient pottery and sculpture red is often used as the colour for the hair and beard. See Cesnola on the bearded Venus, and numerous instances in the vases in the British Museum.

The hair was shorn in sorrow, and severed tresses were hung up as offerings on monuments, and also devoted to the gods in the temples. It was crowned with garlands in joy, and torn out by handfuls in despair. But as the treatment of the heads, hair, and headgear of the ancient Egyptians, Assyrians, Greeks, and other nations will probably form the subject of a separate volume, the matter will not be further dwelt upon here.

Artifices of the Toilet.

References to the painting of the face with white lead by elderly ladies who wished to appear young occur several times in Aristophanes, as in the paragraph on page 34, and the following:—Young man to old woman: "Are you an ape covered over with white lead, or are you an old woman sent up from the dead?" And in another part: "What then? Your alkanet, rather, and your white lead." Alkanet was the Athenian substitute for rouge.

In "Plutus" a young man holds a torch close to the face of an old woman and says: "Oh, see, Poseidon and ye elderly gods, how many wrinkles she has in her face. . . . Upon my word you'd be the better for it if one were to wash you clean." Chremylus says: "Certainly not; for now she is playing the cheat; but if this white lead shall be washed off, you'll see the wrinkles in her face quite plain."

Lysistratè says: "For if we were to sit at home, painted and lightly clad in our vests of fine linen."

In Truculentus, the countryman says: "Because thee hast even presumed to approach our door anointed up with thy unguents, and because thee hast those cheeks, so nicely painted pink." Astaphium replies, "I'troth, it was by reason of your clamour that I coloured in my alarm;" to this Stratilex says, "Thee colour? as though, hussy, thee hadst really left to thy skin the power of receiving any colour. Redden up thy cheeks, thee hast given all thy skin its colour with chalk."

He refers to the woman's false hair in the following terms:—

"If thee doesn't make haste to get away from this with prodigious speed, I'll forthwith be separating, even from thy brains, those falsified, daintily arranged corkscrew curls of thine, with all their grease as well."

Other examples may be found in the Greek Anthology. The following will serve as specimens:—

"You have bought hair, paint, honey, wax, teeth; at the same cost you could have bought a face."—*Palladas.*

"You dye your head; but you will not dye your old age, nor will you stretch out the wrinkles of your cheeks. Do not then plaister the whole of your face with paint, so that you have a mask, and not a face. For it is of no use. Why are you mad? A paint and wash will never make a Hecuba a Helen."—*Lucian.*

"Themistonoé, thrice as old as a crow, after dyeing her white hair, has become on a sudden not youth-like, but Rhea-like."—*Lucian.*

According to Theocritus, the following touching accident occurred in a respectable family in Alexandria two or three hundred years before the Christian era. The good-wife says: "Papa indeed lately (and we call everything lately, you know), going to buy nitre and ceruse from a stall, brought home salt instead, the great big oaf." The nitre and paints of various colours were to be used for the dresses and cheeks of the women. "Nec cerussa tibi nec nitri spuma rubentis desit."

In Mostellaria there is an elaborate description of a woman's toilet. Philematium calls for the mirror, the casket with her trinkets, the ceruse—that is cerussa, or white lead, for whitening the complexion—then she asks for the rouge; but the flattering waiting-woman replies: "I shan't give it. You are really a clever one. Do you wish to patch up a most excellent picture with a new daubing? It's not right that any paint should touch your body—neither ceruse, nor quince ointment, nor any other wash. . . . A woman smells best when she smells of nothing at all. For those old women who are in the habit of anointing themselves with unguents, vamped-up creatures, old hags, and toothless, who hide the blemishes of the person with paint; when the sweat has blended itself with the unguents, forthwith they stink just as when a cook has poured together a variety of broths; what they smell of you don't know, except this only, that you understand that badly they do smell." In reply to the question of gold trinkets, this philosophic waiting-woman says, that it does not befit her mistress to concern herself about them. "Age is to be enveloped in purple; gold ornaments are unsuitable for a woman. A beautiful woman will be more beautiful naked than drest in purple. Besides it's in vain she's well drest if she's ill-conducted; ill conduct soils fine ornaments worse than dirt. But if she's beauteous, she's sufficiently adorned."

Even the admirable young wife of Ischomachus is not without a weakness for paints, for we read in Xenophon's "Good Husbandry" the following conversation:—

"'Go on, I pray you, good Ischomachus,' said Socrates; 'for it is far more delightful to hear the virtues of a good woman described, than if the famous painter Zeuxis was to show me the portrait of the fairest woman in the world.' 'Then,' continued Ischomachus, 'I remember, on a particular day, she had painted her face with a certain cosmetic, attempting to make her skin look fairer than it was; and with another mixture had endeavoured to increase the natural bloom of her cheeks; and also had put on higher shoes than ordinary, to make her look taller than she naturally was. When I perceived this,' said Ischomachus, 'I saluted her in the following manner:—"Tell me, good wife, which would make me the most acceptable in your eyes, to deal sincerely by you, in delivering into your possession those things which are really my own, without making more of my estate than it is; or for me to deceive you, by producing a thousand falsities which have nothing in them; giving you chains of brass instead of gold, false jewels, false money, and false purple, instead of that which is true and genuine." To which she presently replied, "May the gods forbid that you should be such a man! for, should you harbour such deceit in your heart, I should never love you." "I tell you then, dear wife," replied Ischomachus, "we are come together, to love one another, and to delight in each other's perfections; do you think I should be the more agreeable to you in my person, or should you love me the better, if I was to put a false lustre upon myself, that I might appear better complexioned, more fair in body, or more manly than what nature has made me; or that I should paint and anoint my face when you receive me to your arms, and give you this deceit instead of my natural person?" "Surely, dear Ischomachus," replied his wife, "your own person in its natural perfection is preferable to all the paints and ointments you can use to set it off; nor can all the art you might use be comparable to your natural appearance." "Believe then, good wife," said Ischomachus, "that I have the same abhorrence of false lustre that you have; can there be anything more complete in nature than yourself? or would there be anything less engaging to me than that you should use any means to hide or destroy those perfections in you which I so much admire? The God of nature has appointed beauties in all creatures, as well in the field as among the human race; the magnificence of the male to be admired by the female, and the tender and curious texture of the female to be admired by the male. It is natural for the creatures in the field to

distinguish one another by the purity of their beauties; there is no deceit, there is no corruption; so the men always admire that body which is most pure or the least deformed by art. Such wiles and deceits may, perhaps, deceive strangers, because they will not have opportunities of discovering and laughing at them; but if such things should be practised between those who are daily conversant with one another, how soon will the imposition be discovered? How soon will they be ridiculed? For these deceits appear at the rising out of bed, and from that time till the persons have had opportunity of renewing them; as well as when they sweat, when they shed tears, when they wash, and when they bathe themselves."'
'What answer, good Ischomachus,' said Socrates, 'did your wife give you to this lecture?' 'The best that could be,' replied Ischomachus, 'for she has never since attempted any of these false glosses, but has constantly appeared in her natural beauties, and repeated her solicitations to me to instruct her, if there was any natural means of assisting them. I then directed her that she should not sit too much, but exercise herself about the house as a mistress, to examine how her several works went forward; sometimes to go among the spinners or weavers, to see that they did their duty, and to instruct those who were ignorant, and encourage the most deserving among them; sometimes to look into the bakehouse, to see the neatness and order of the woman that looks after it; and sometimes visit her housekeeper, to account with her for the yarn or other commodities that are brought into her charge; and now and then to take a turn about her house, to see that everything is disposed

in its proper place. This method, I suppose,' said Ischomachus, 'would be a means of giving her a healthful exercise, and at the same time of leading her to that business which would be for her advantage, in benefiting our fortune. I also told her the exercise of cooking, baking, and looking after the furniture of her house, to brush it and keep it clean, when she wanted something to do, would be commendable, and help to employ her; for I recommended exercise to her as a great benefit; for exercise,' said Ischomachus, 'will create you an appetite to your meat, and by that means you will be more healthful, and add, if possible, to the bloom of your beauty; and also the clean appearance of the mistress among the servants, and her readiness to set her hand to work, will encourage them to follow her example; for a good example does more than all the compulsion that can be used. Those who study nothing but their dress may indeed be esteemed by those who understand nothing else; but the outside appearance is deceitful. And now, good Socrates, I have a wife who lives up to the rules given her.'"

Another refinement of the Athenian ladies who wished to pass for beauties was the removing of hairs from the armpits and other parts of the body. This was sometimes done by plucking, at others by singeing. For an example of the first, see Lysistrata, 150: "Having the hairs plucked off our bosoms." Of the second, see allusion in the opening lines of the Ecclesiazusæ, where Praxagora, addressing the lamp, says: "And you cast light on our persons when you singe off the hair which flourishes upon them."

Miscellaneous.

According to one of Solon's laws, the bride was to bring with her only three suits of clothes and some household stuff of small value, so that marriages should not be mercenary.

By other laws of Solon, women are forbidden to travel with more than three gowns, or more meat and drink than they can purchase for an obolus; "neither shall they carry with them more than a hand-basket, or go anywhere at night but in a chariot with a lamp or torch before it. Courtesans shall wear flowered garments to distinguish them from virtuous women. No adulteress shall be permitted to adorn herself; she that doth, shall have her garments cut or torn off her back by any one that meets her; she shall likewise be beaten, though not so as to be killed or disabled."

Harlots in primitive times covered their faces with veils or masks.

Suppliants at the temples or altars often clothed themselves with rags, or put on the habit of mourners, to move pity and compassion.

The juror who was required to swear in the temple of Ceres and Proserpine, or Ceres Thesmophorus, after the performance of certain ceremonies, was clothed in the purple vestment of the goddess, and holding a lighted torch in his hand, as being in the presence of the Deity, took oath by all the gods in the world. This the Syracusans accounted the most solemn and sacred oath that could be.

The priestesses of Apollo at Delphi were at first young virgins; in later times they were chosen from women over fifty years of age, yet they wore the habit of virgins, to signify their purity and virgin modesty. They were not allowed to clothe themselves in rich and costly apparel, to use fantastic dress, to wear purple garments, or to anoint themselves with perfumes. Before sitting on the tripod the priestess or Pythia used to wash her whole body, and particularly her hair, in the Castalian fountain.

Articles of female attire were offered up in the temples. Their kind and quality are indicated in the following extract from the Anthology:—

"These sandals that keep the feet warm, the delightful labour of skilful shoemakers, has Bitenna offered up; and Philonis this binder of the hair, that loves to be plaited, a cap dyed in the colour of the bright sea; and Anticlea, the fan; and the lovely Heliodora, the veil for the face, a work partaking of the spider's web; but she, who has a name called after her father Aristotle, the serpent with pretty folds, an ornament of gold for her slim ankles; all of one mind and age have given these presents to the heavenly Cythéra-born Aphrodité."

Antipater of Sidon.

The parasol and umbrella were well known in Athens. In the procession of the Panathenœa, the select virgins, who were the basket-bearers, or κανηφόροι, were attended by girls of inferior rank, who carried their umbrellas and little seats. Aristophanes refers in several places to the parasol, Thesmop. 825, &c. In "The Birds" we read:—

"(*Enter Prometheus, muffled up, and covered with an umbrella.*) . . . But in order that I may run away back again, bring my umbrella, so that even if Jove should see me from above, I may appear to be attending on a Canephorus."

The Greeks and Romans sometimes used the hanging corner of the himation or toga to wipe the sweat from their brows (*see* Mercator, ver. 136); but it is not improbable that the classical equivalent to the modern pocket-handkerchief was also in use. In Juvenal, a man addresses his wife in something like the following words: "You are offensive. You use your handkerchief too much; a new wife is coming with a dry nose."

The sandal was often one of the most costly articles of the female dress, being much adorned with gold and embroidery. Originally it was worn by both sexes, and consisted of a wooden sole, fastened with thongs to the foot. In later times its use was confined to females; a piece of leather covered the toes, while thongs elegantly decorated were attached to it. Shoes were also used; and clogs, part wood and part leather, or entirely of wood, like the sabots of the Continent, were worn by slaves.

In the Banquet of Xenophon reference is made to the agility and intelligence of the dancing-girls (*see* plates 19, 20, 109 to 112) :—

Fig. 33.

"Immediately Ariadné entered the room, richly dressed in the habit of a bride, and placed herself in the elbow chair."

"Then a hoop being brought in with swords fixed all around it, their points upwards, and placed in the middle of the hall, the dancing-girl immediately leaped head foremost into it through the midst of the points, and then out again with a wonderful agility."

"I see the dancing-girl entering at the other end of the hall, and she has brought her cymbals along with her."

At the same time the other girl took her flute; the one played and the other danced to admiration; the dancing-girl throwing up and catching again her cymbals, so as to answer exactly the cadency of the music, and that with a surprising dexterity.

The costume of female acrobats is indicated in fig. 33, in which the lower limbs of the figure are shown enveloped in thin drawers. Other vase paintings show that female acrobatic costume sometimes consisted solely of a decorated band swathed round the abdomen and upper part of the thighs, thus resembling in appearance the middle band adopted by modern acrobats.

LIST OF ILLUSTRATIONS.

Plate
1. Figure wearing diplax or mantle doubled over the chiton poderes, or chiton reaching to the feet.
2. Figure with long-sided chiton.
3. Figure with diploïdion or bib over peplos and chiton poderes.
4. Figure with ampechonion or outer garment, and sleeveless chiton buttoned to give the appearance of sleeves.
5. Priestess of Demeter (Ceres) with long-sided diploïdion or ampechonion.
6. Side view of figure with detached diploïdion.
7. Demeter (Ceres) with clasp-fastened chiton and veil (kredemnon).
8, 9, 10. Girls with clasp-fastened chitons; the upper part is doubled over, and the girdle goes over the two thicknesses of the cloth.
11. Priestess of Demeter wearing simplest form of chiton girt at the waist; the upper part hangs over in front as a diploïdion.
12. Female with chiton arranged with long sides, upper part folded over in front.
13. Priestess with chiton and veil (kredemnon).
14, 15. Figures wearing chitons with upper part folded over as a bib, and fastened at the shoulders by clasps.
16. Bacchante with sacred fillet and thyrsus; chiton folded over and girt over the two thicknesses of cloth.
17. Figure with chiton, upper part hanging over to give the effect of a second garment.
18. Girl with chiton made of one large piece of cloth; it is embroidered on the upper or diploïdion part to represent a bib.
19. Bacchante with the crotals, dancing, showing the opening at the sides of the garment.

LIST OF ILLUSTRATIONS.

Plate
20. Female dancer with himation only, called, when thus worn, achiton, i.e. without chiton.
21. Bacchante with thyrsus, wears chiton over girt diploïdion, and scarf (μαντιλη, mantilè).
22. Bacchante with crotals, wears single chiton without doubled part, and scarf (mantilè).
23. Bacchante with torches, wearing himation, or cloak.
24. Bacchante with rod of sesamum, wearing chiton and himation.
25. Female flute-player, wearing chiton and himation.
26. Mourner, wears chiton, and has part of himation wrapped round the head as a veil.
27. Electra, with shorn hair, wears dark embroidered chiton and himation.
28. Canephoros, i.e. maiden who bore a basket containing offerings for Athénè in the solemn procession of Panathenæa at Athens. Wears *probably* white and gold embroidered chiton and himation.
29. Lady with mirror, wears wide-sleeved chiton and himation.
30. Leaning figure, wears chiton and himation.
31. Figure with chiton and himation.
32, 33. Figures, each with double chiton, and putting on himation.
34. Leaning figure wearing chiton and himation.
35. Leaning figure wearing himation as achiton, or without chiton.
36. Erato wearing chiton arranged to cover the arm, also a himation.
37. Figure with chiton and himation.
38. Lady with himation, arranged double, diplax or diploïs.
39. Hérè (Juno) wearing himation as a diplax, that is two-ply, the lower only partly covered by the upper ply.
40. Figure wearing himation so as to show the two thicknesses of the cloth (diploïs).
41. Figure with chiton and himation.
42. Figure with chiton, himation, and veil (kredemnon).
43. Demeter (Ceres) with the himation worn as a diplax.
44. Demeter (Ceres) with double-girded chiton and himation.
45. Demeter (Ceres) with himation or peplos partly twisted round the body as a girdle, and partially covering the head as a veil.
46. Hygeia with himation or cloak partly twisted round the body as a girdle.

LIST OF ILLUSTRATIONS.

Plate
47. Figure with mantle partly girt round the waist.
48. Cybelê wears himation worn round the body and over the head as a veil.
49. Clio wears himation enveloping the whole figure.
50. Euterpe with chiton girt at the breast.
51. Muse with wide chiton.
52. Erato, in achiton, that is, with himation serving both as chiton and cloak.
53. Low-girded Danaïd.
54. Figure wearing double-girded chiton.
55, 56. Artemis (Diana) wearing chiton double-girded, and kilted above the knee.
57. Artemis wearing chiton girt up with scarf or peplos.
58. Artemis with skirts let down to the ground; she also wears a veil (parapatasma, skepasma, peripetasma, prokalumma) over her shoulders. In Homer the head veil is called kredemnon.
59. Artemis (Diana) wearing the detached diploïdion over the chiton.
60. Pallas Athéné (Minerva) wearing the ægis with the Gorgon's head on her breast; she wears the himation as a diplax. This statue answers the description of the Athéné of Phidias, in the Parthenon (see also plate 71).
61. Athéné with peplos or himation partly girt round the waist.
62. Athéné wearing chiton, upper girt diploïdion, and himation or parapatasma hanging from the shoulders.
63. Athéné (Minerva) in the diplax.
64. Juno Lanuvina, or Athéné, wearing the goat's skin, Αἰγέη, hence Αἰγὶς, Ægis.
65. Statue of Athéné; wears as under-garment the chiton, next the peplos, with the wars of the giants embroidered thereon; the upper part of the garment is turned over at the neck, so as to hang over the under portion, and so form a diploïdion, or this diploïdion may be made of a separate piece of cloth. Over all she wears the ægis, or skin of the goat Amalthea, which was fastened over the shoulders and breast, and hung over the left arm as a shield-cover (see plate 66). Afterwards it was used solely as a breastplate (see plates 60, 61, 68). The breast part of the ægis has the Gorgon's head.

F 2

LIST OF ILLUSTRATIONS.

Plate
66. Athéné. The peplos and diploïdion, and the Gorgoned ægis extended as a covering to the arm that holds the shield.
67. The Æginetan Athéné wears diploïdion, peplos, and the ægis.
68. Athéné wearing ægis with Gorgon's head as a breastplate.
69. *a.* Torso of Athéné, with Gorgoned ægis fastened round the waist by a girdle of lion's skin with head attached. *b.* Athéné of Velletri wearing the diplax. *c.* Athéné with the ægis as a breastplate, with serpent girdle over diploïdion—early period.
70. Three representations of Athéné in war attire. *b* shows the ægis, or goat's skin, fastened over the right shoulder, and going diagonally across the body under the left armpit. In *c*, Athéné wears the himation over the ægis.
71. Three representations of Athéné in war dress.
72. Two representations of Athéné, from early pottery.
73. Eight representations of Athéné—various periods.
74. Héré (Juno) wearing transparent chiton and two-ply himation or diplax.
75. Three representations of Héré (Juno), showing the chiton, himation, and veil (kredemnon).
76. Three representations of Demeter (Ceres).
77. Two representations of Demeter, sitting.
78. Figure of Antiochia, from the statue by Eutychides of Sicyon.
79. Artemis (Diana) wearing long chiton and veil.
80. Three representations of Artemis.
81. Dress of the third period of Greek art history. The chief figures represented are Amphitrite, Hestia, Hermes, Artemis, Heracles, from early painted pottery.
82. The upper line represents Demeter, Hecaté, Triptolemus, and others. The lower shows Artemis, Leto, Aphrodité, and others, in the early Ionian style of dress.
83. Female dress of the time of Phidias, from the Panathenæan procession on the frieze of the Parthenon.
84. The upper group represents Apollo, Artemis, Heracles, and Athéné—early middle style of dress. The lower shows Persephone (inscribed Περοφατα), Triptolemus, and Demeter, also in early middle style of dress.
85. Upper group shows Aphrodite, Hera, and Demeter, from the early sculpture of the Altar of the Twelve Gods. The lower

LIST OF ILLUSTRATIONS.   85

Plate

group is of the same early period, and shows various modes of wearing the himation.
86. Upper group shows Aphroditè, Artemis, Hephaistos, and Athéné. The lower group shows an uncommon arrangement of the diploïdion.
87. The two larger figures are Leto and Artemis. The smaller figures belong to a different time and district, and represent the richly embroidered dresses of the Heroic period.
88. Figures wearing the dress of the Bacchic festivals (Dionysia).
89. Figures in various styles of chitons.
90. Priestess, attendant, and Héré—old style.
91. Artemis, allegorical figure, and Hébè.
92. Various modes of wearing the himation.
93. Chitons and himations.
94. Large himations.
95. Mourning females.
96. Early Lycian or Ionian style of dress.
97. Greek female dressed in monochiton, or in the chiton without himation.
98. Female with lyre and plectrum.
99. Lady with umbrella.
100, 101, 102. Greek ladies sitting.
103. Greek lady and attendants.
104. Greek ladies—early style of dress.
105. Aphroditè, Muse, Artemis.
106. Artemis, Demeter, Aphroditè.
107. Héré attired in various ways.
108. Figures of the Muses and of Artemis.
109, 110, 111, 112. Dancing females, showing various arrangements of the chiton, diploïdion, and himation.

CUTS IN THE LETTERPRESS.

Fig.		Page
Head of Bacchante	. . . . .	Title-page
1. Dorian or Early Greek male and female costume	. .	6
2. Nausicaa and her maids, from early Greek pottery	. .	7

LIST OF ILLUSTRATIONS.

Fig.		Page
3.	Virgin wearing short chiton	11
4.	Spartan virgin wearing chitoniskos	11
5.	Dorian female costume	14
6.	Lycian dresses from the Xanthus sculptures. This kind of dress formed the model for Ionian and late Greek dresses.	16
7.	The early long-chiton with upper part doubled over to form a bib, fastened at the shoulders by gold clasps	19
8.	Early chiton, open entirely at the side (*see* page 13)	20
9.	Caryatide showing the chiton poderes, or chiton reaching to the feet, with the middle part puffed over the girdle, and the upper part hanging as a bib	20
10.	Figures wearing chitons and detached diploïdions or ampechonions	22
11.	Figure of Artemis wearing the χιτὼν ποδήρης, or chiton reaching to the feet, and over it the ampechonion	23
12.	Simple chiton fastened at the shoulders	26
13.	The ampechonion arranged as a diploïd (two-ply) bib	26
14.	Early figure with chiton poderes and large ampechonion	27
15.	The ampechonion arranged as a single bib, imitating the upper hanging part of the early chiton	27
16.	Figure with chiton and outer garment or himation. Hope calls this outer garment the peplum. The words peplos and peploma signify a robe or garment. The peplos of Athéné on which the wars of the giants were embroidered, was not an outer garment, but one worn over the chiton but under the diploïdion or himation (*see* plate 65)	28
17.	Figure from old vase painting representing the taking of Troy. This cut shows the Eastern light diaphanous dresses largely adopted in Greece in later times	40
18.	Richly embroidered dress, Phrygian style, in use among the Greeks of South Italy	45
19.	Figure of Artemis with embroidered petticoat, from a vase painting in the British Museum	46
20.	Lady working at embroidery frame	47
21.	Bracelet from Ilios	51
22.	Golden diadem from Mycenæ	51
23.	Figure of Aphroditè wearing chiton and embroidered himation	56
24.	Figure of Aphroditè wearing chiton and ampechonion	57

LIST OF ILLUSTRATIONS.

Fig.		Page
25.	Héré, from early sculpture on the Altar of the Twelve Gods	58
26.	Athéné, from vase painting in the British Museum	60
27.	Ditto ditto ditto	61
28.	Athéné with ægis covering left arm (*see also* plate 66)	62
29, 30.	Bacchantes, from vase paintings in the British Museum	65, 66
31.	Bacchante, from Hope's "Costumes"	67
32.	Bacchante, from the British Museum	68
33.	Female juggler	79
34.	Bacchante	80
35.	Head of Greek lady	81
36.	Head of Athéné, from the Temple at Ægina	87
37.	Athéné pleading before Zeus	88

Athéné, from the pediment of the Temple at Ægina.

Athéné pleading before Zeus.

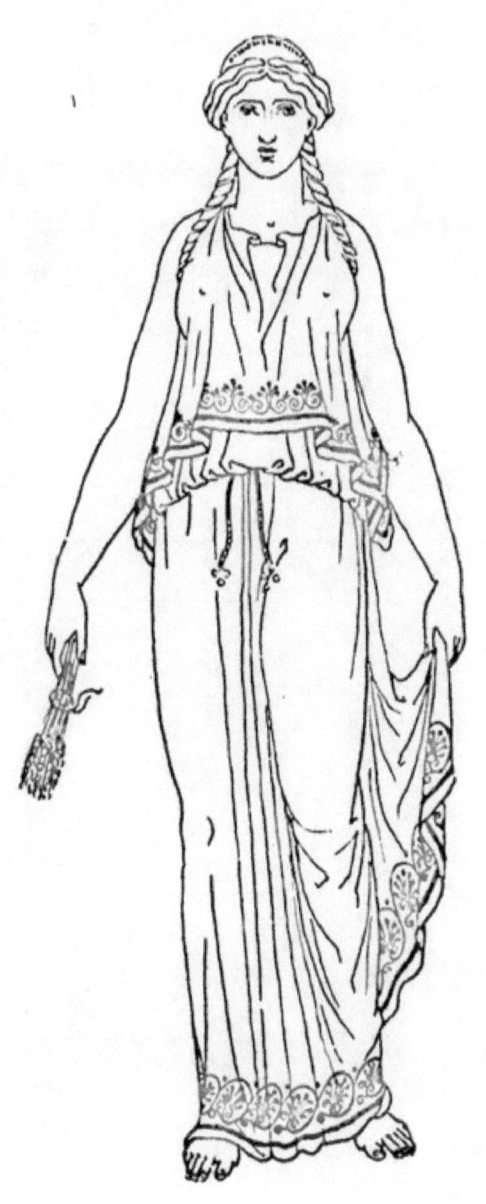

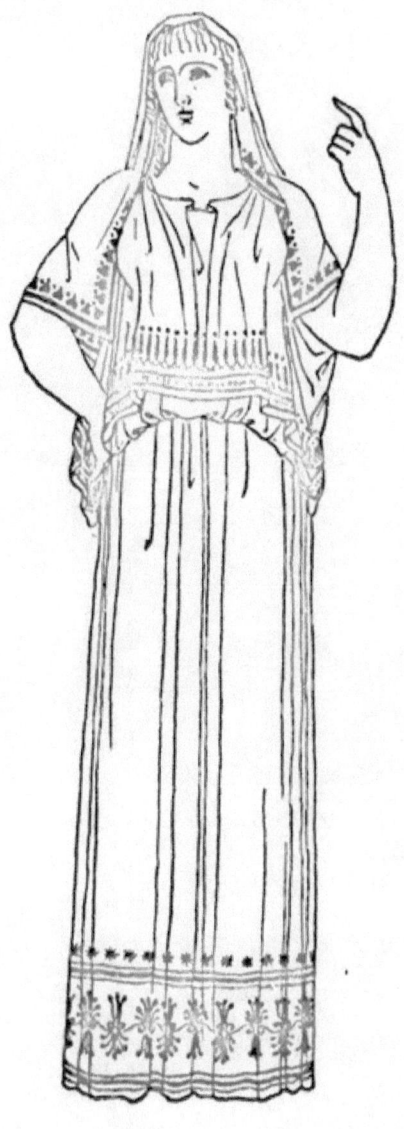

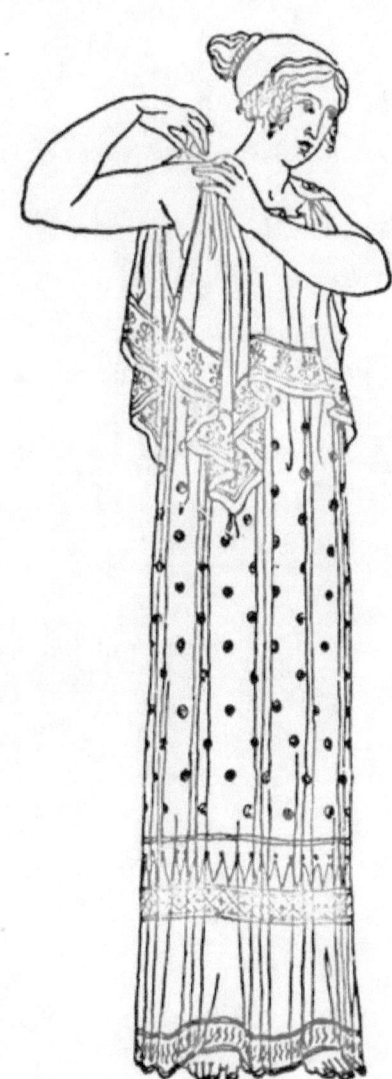

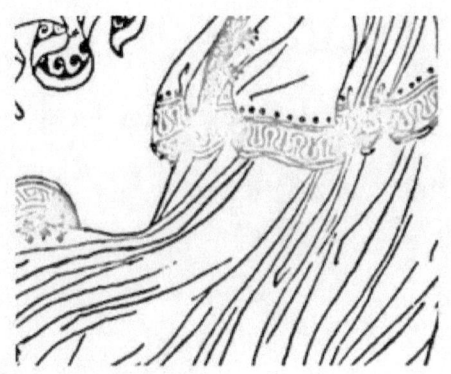

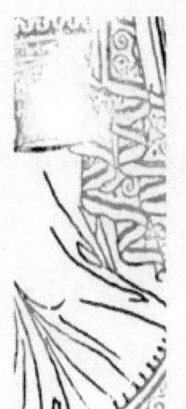

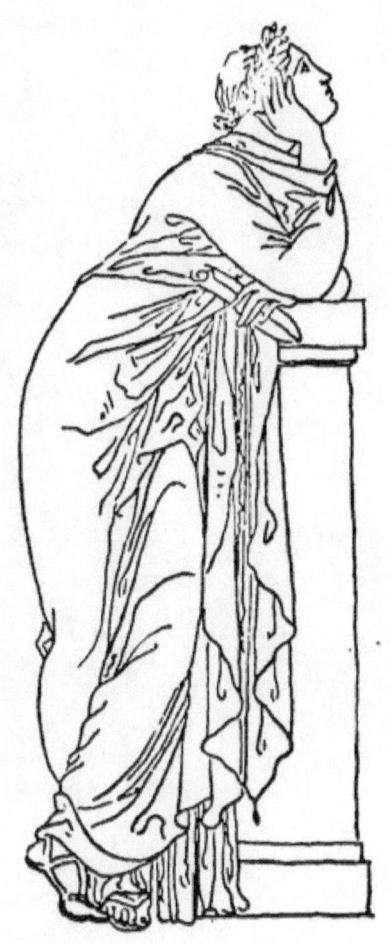

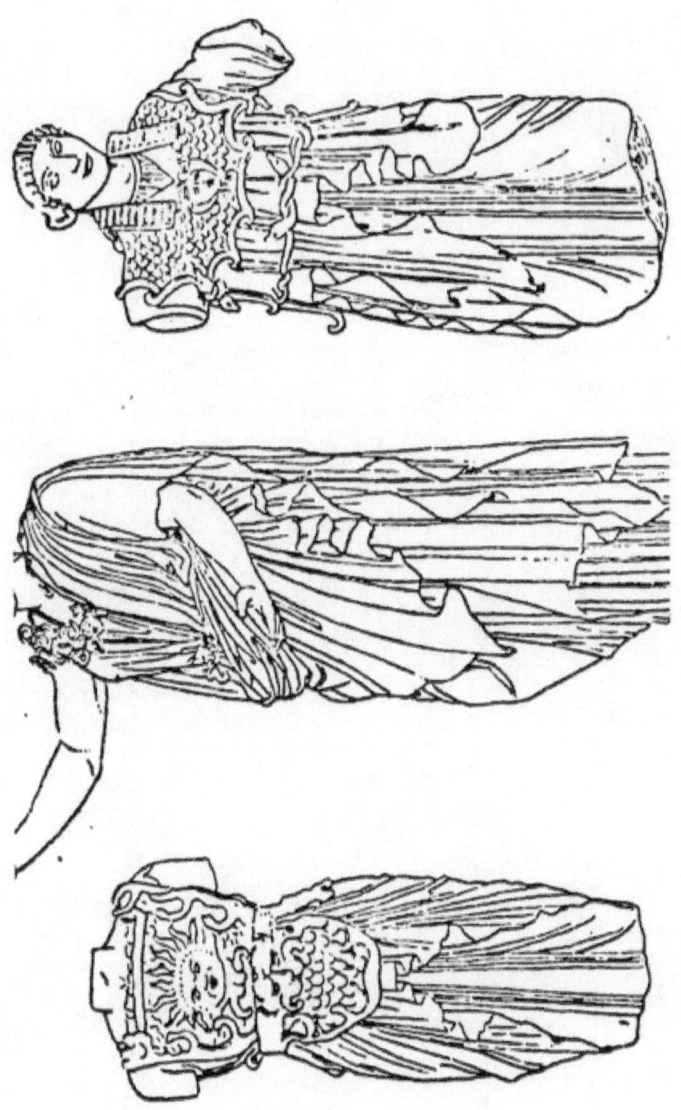

70

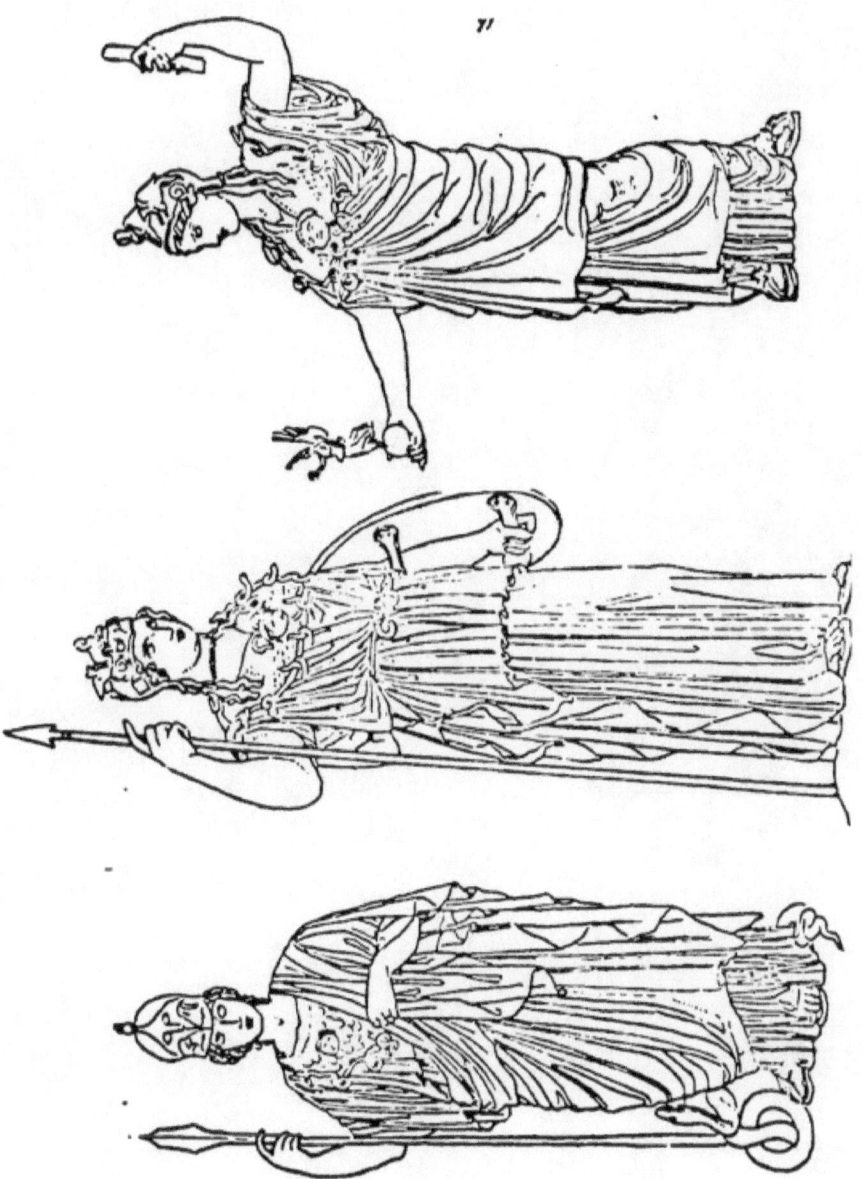

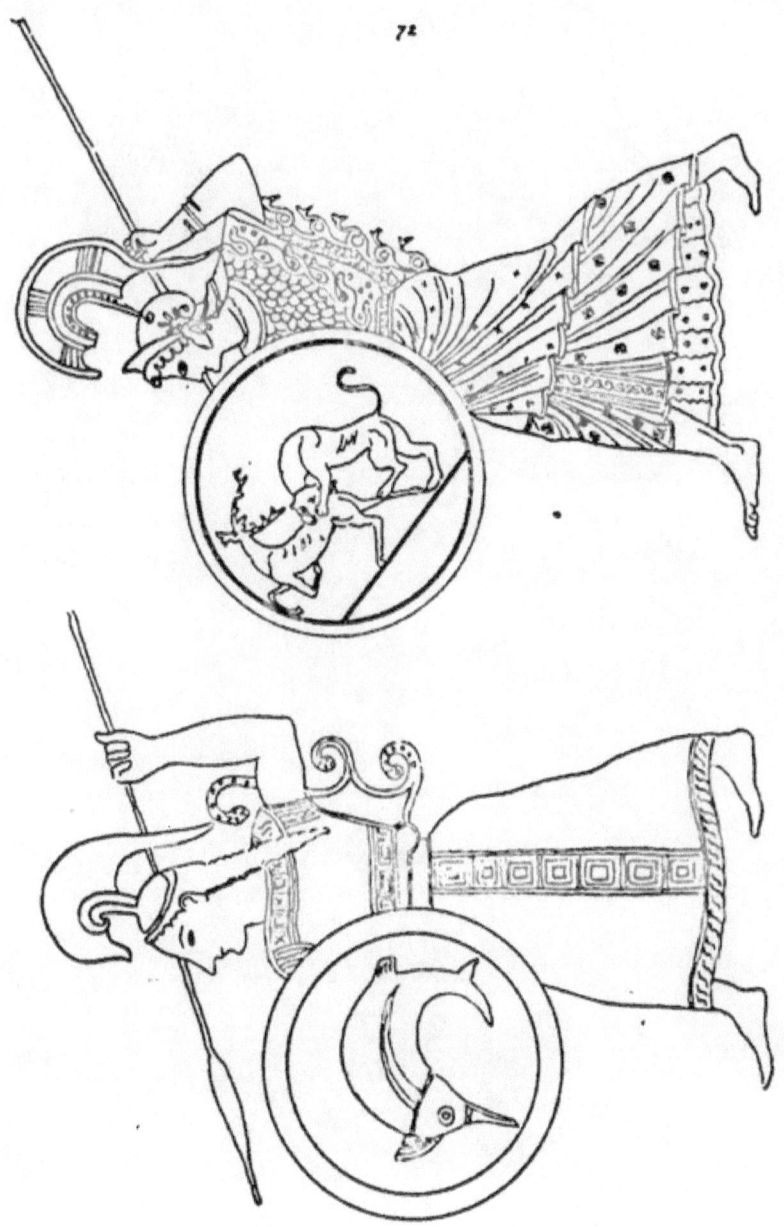

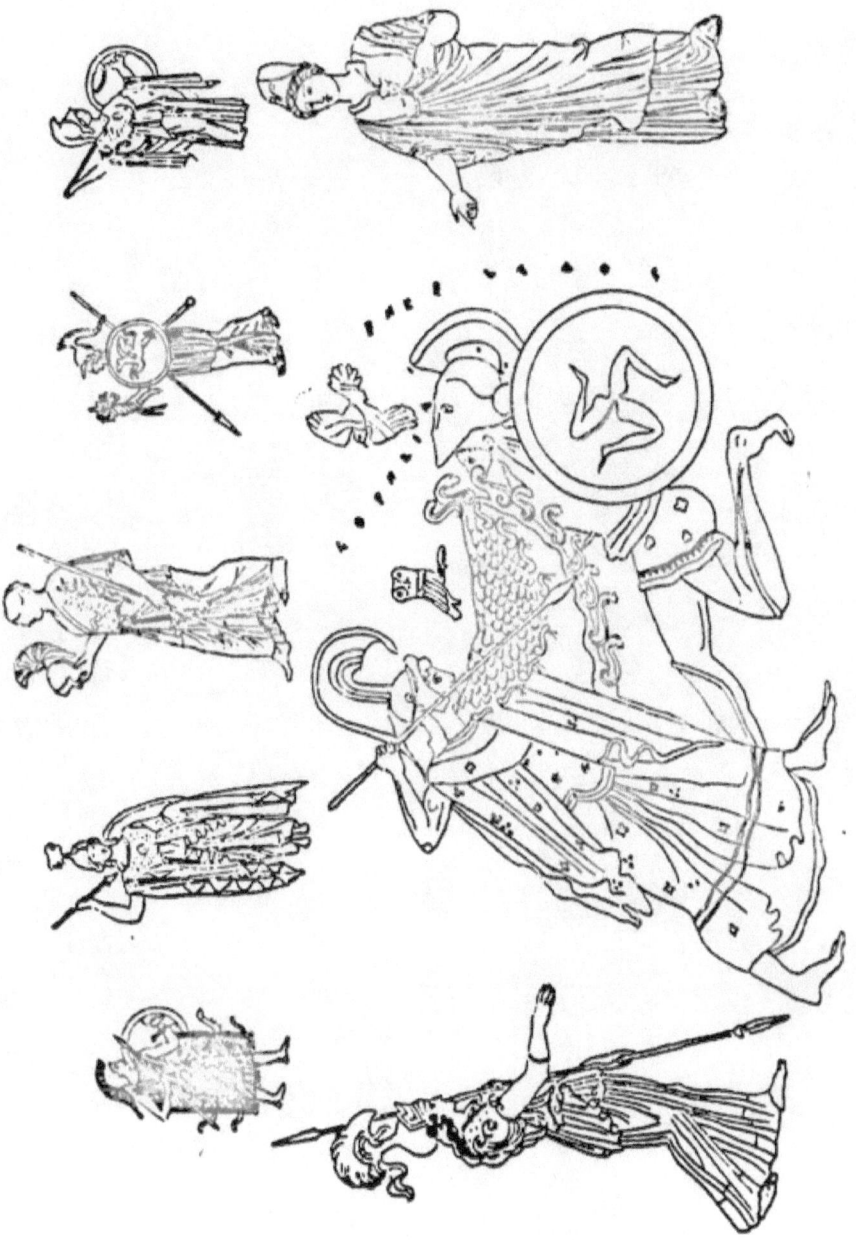

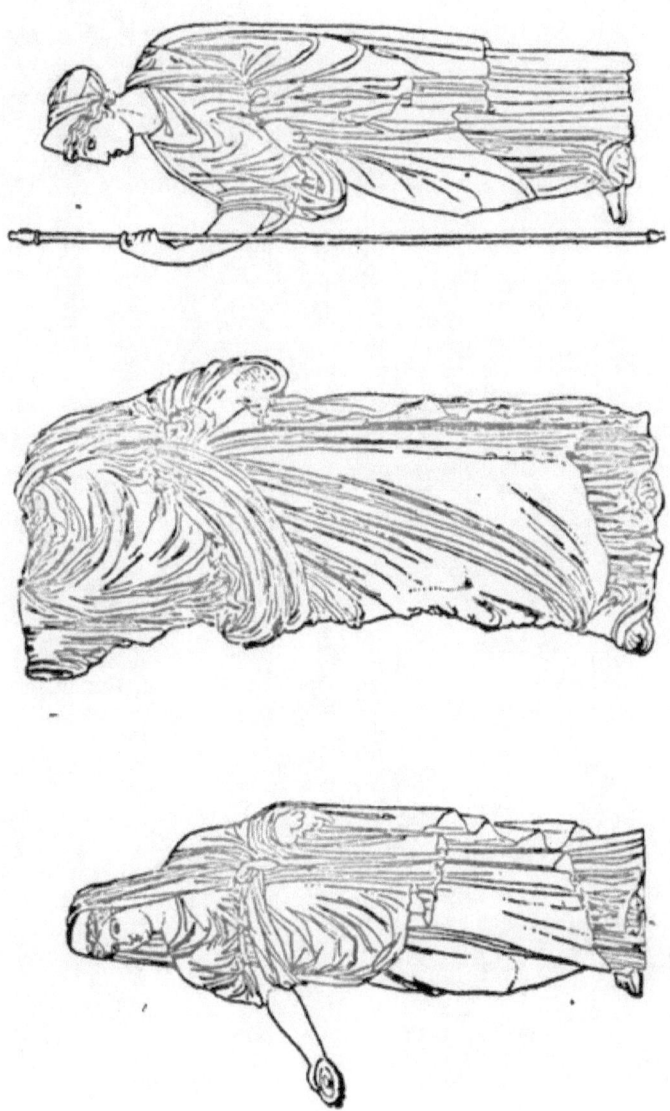

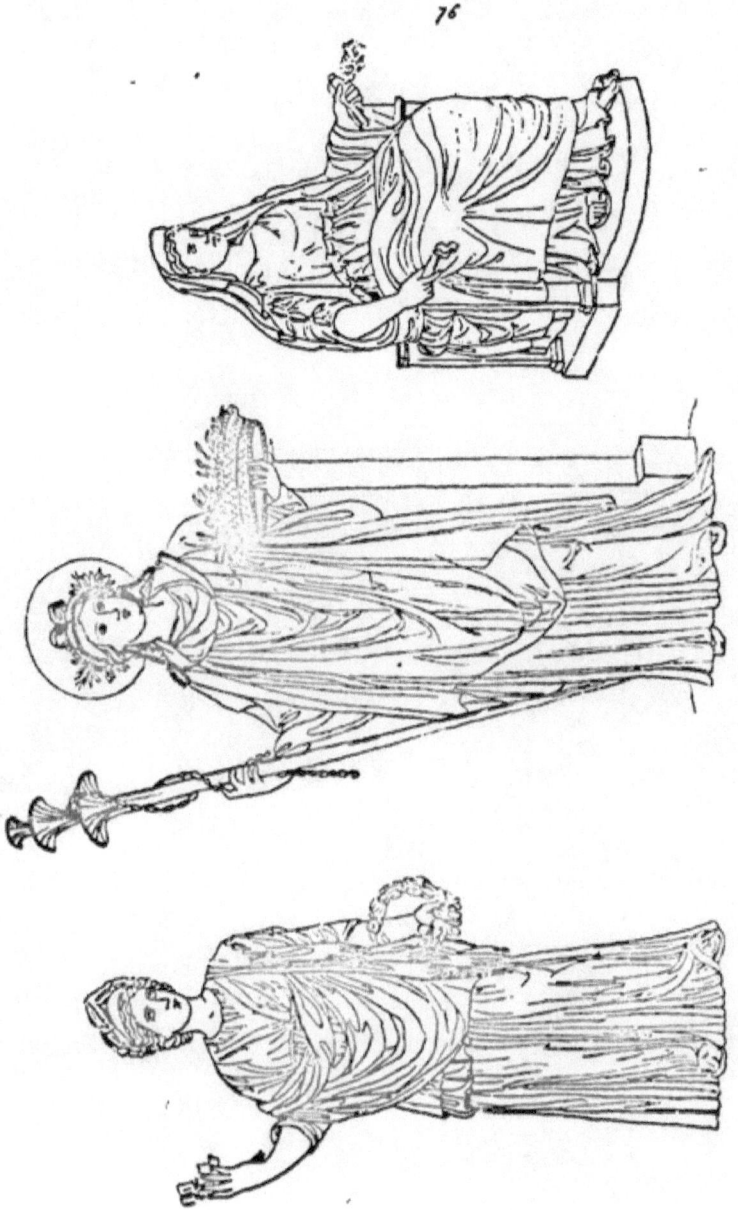

77

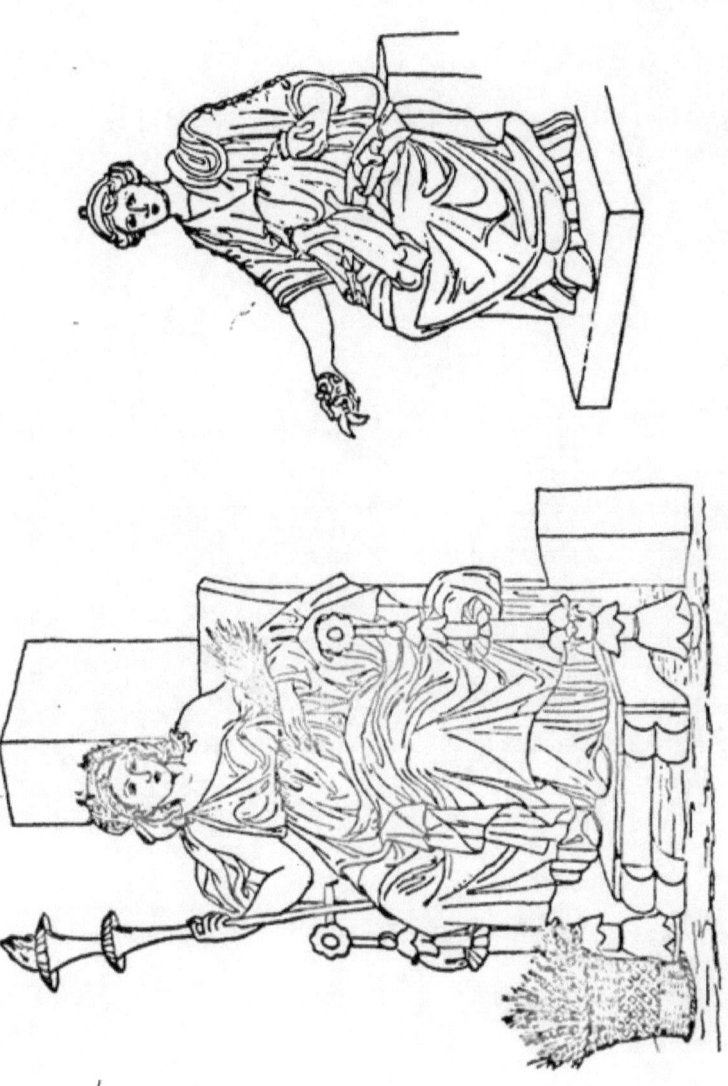

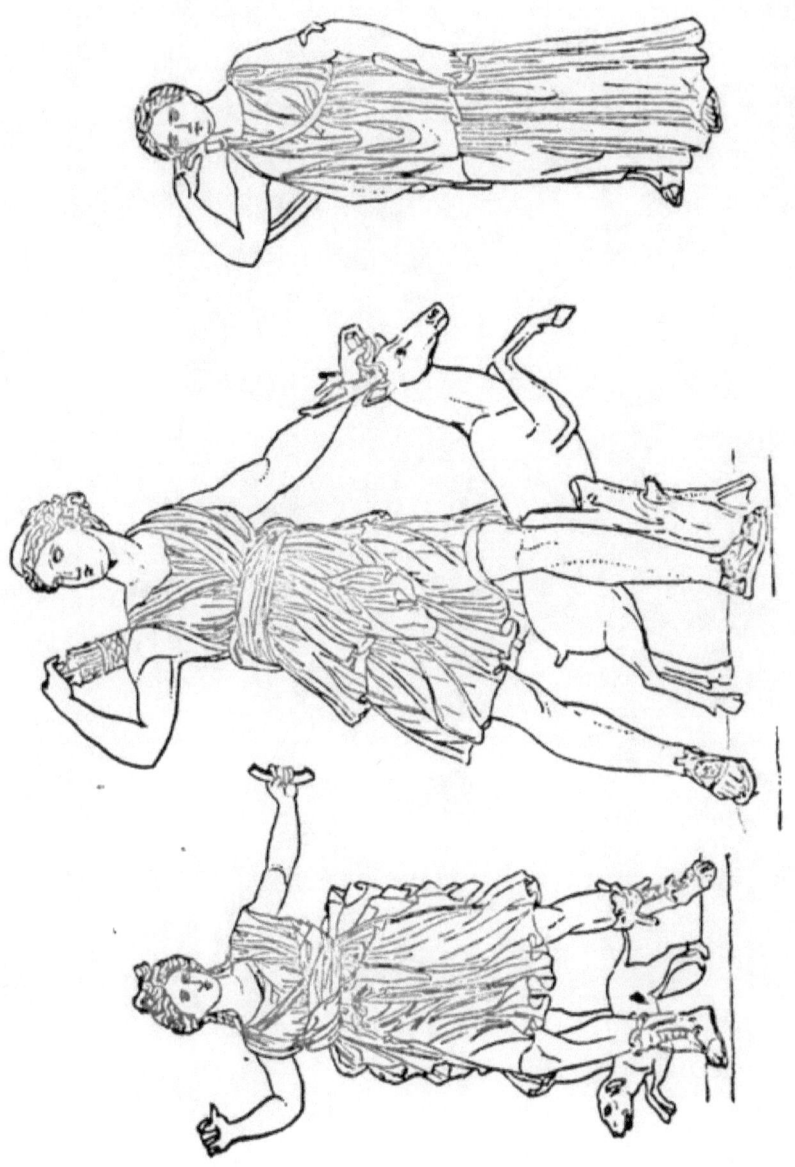

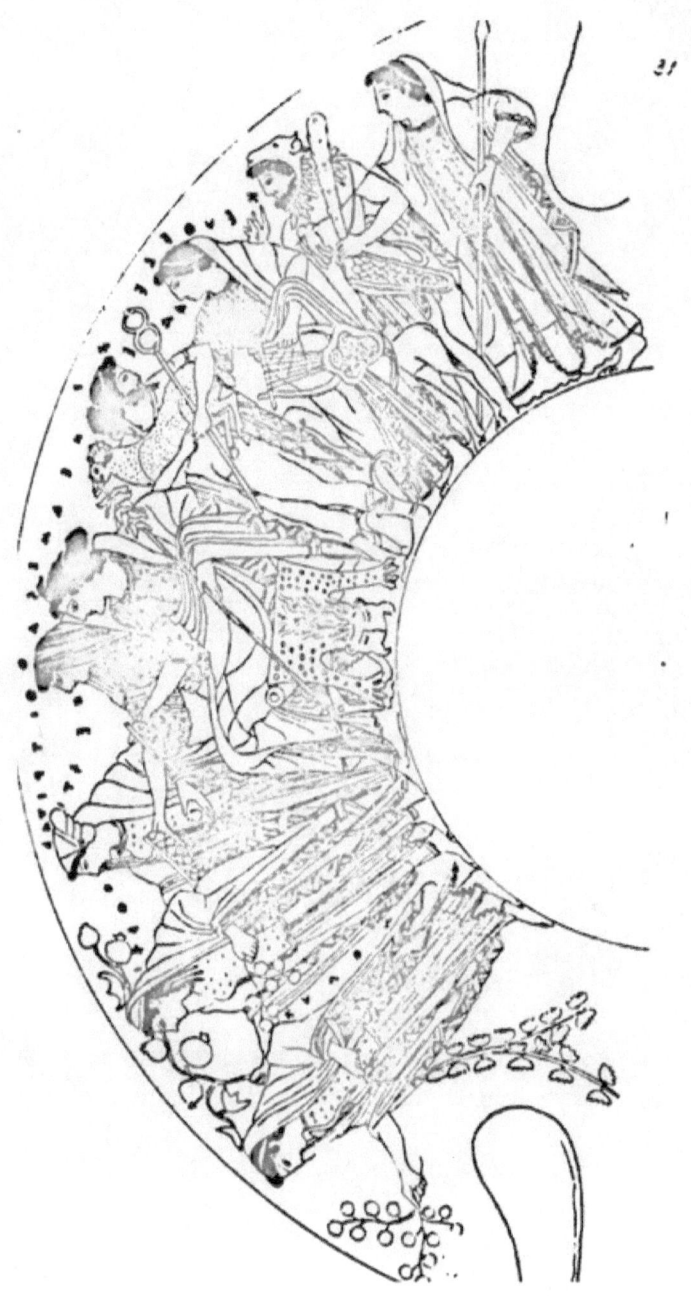

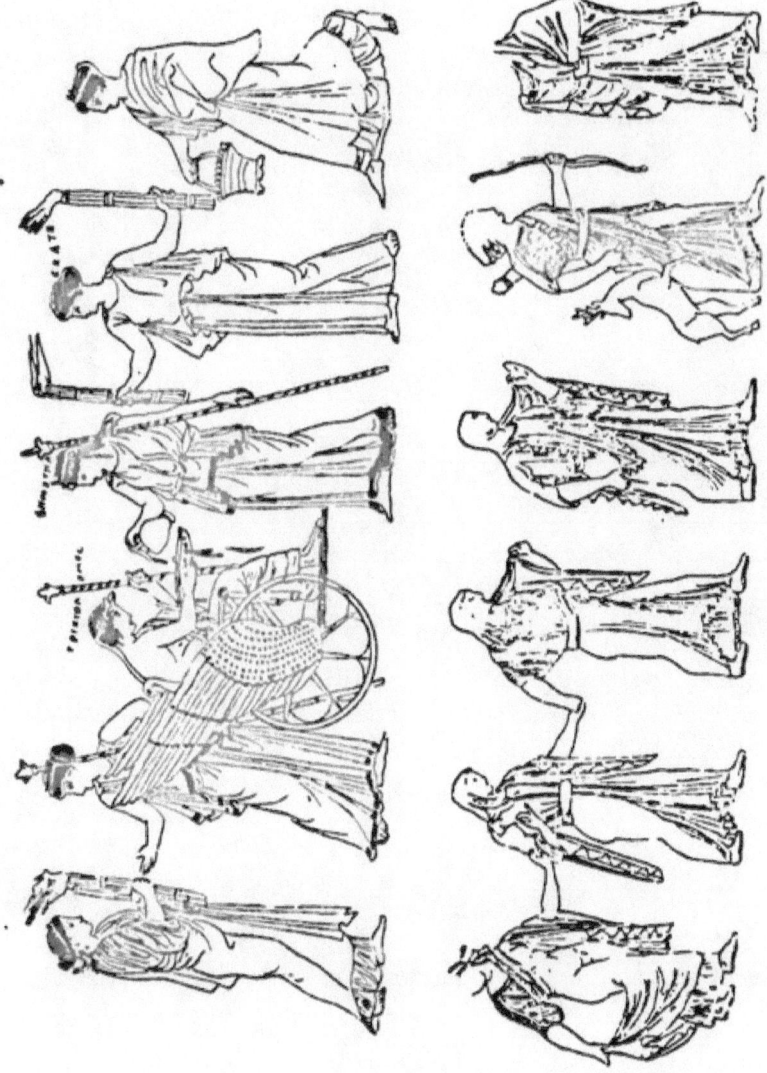

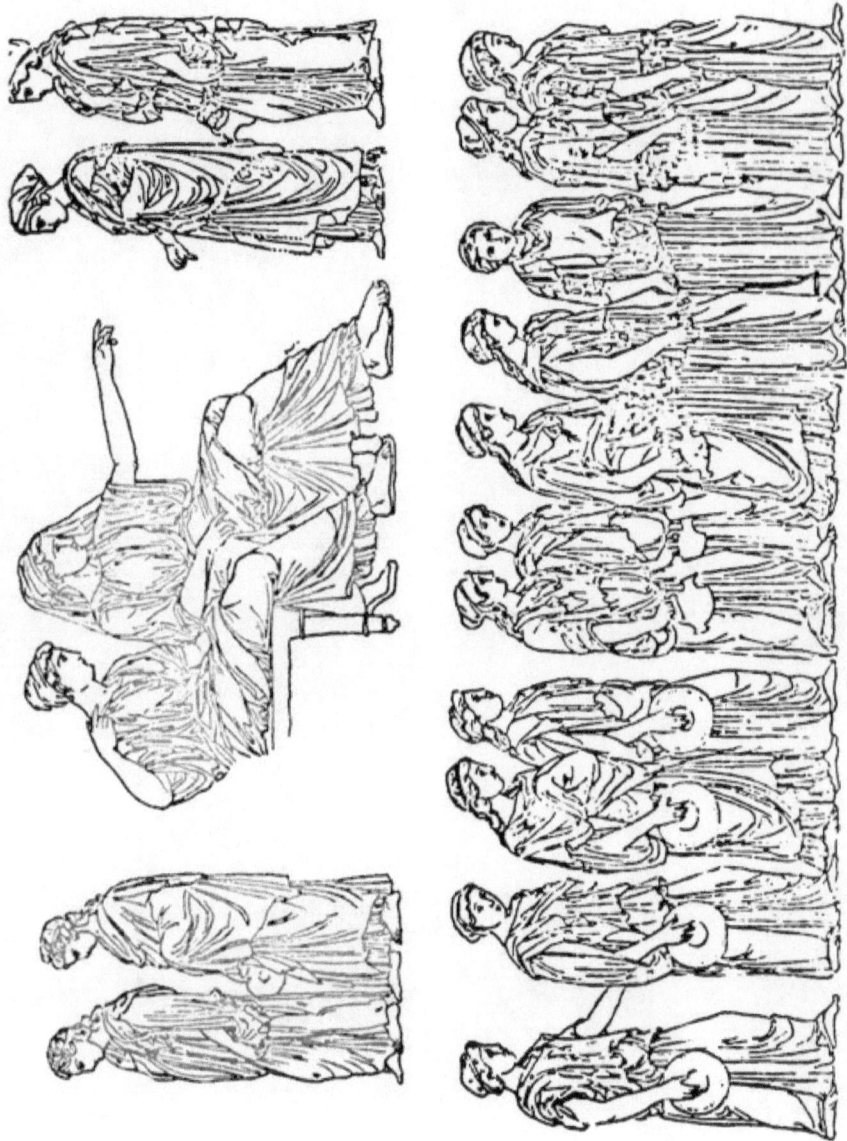

83

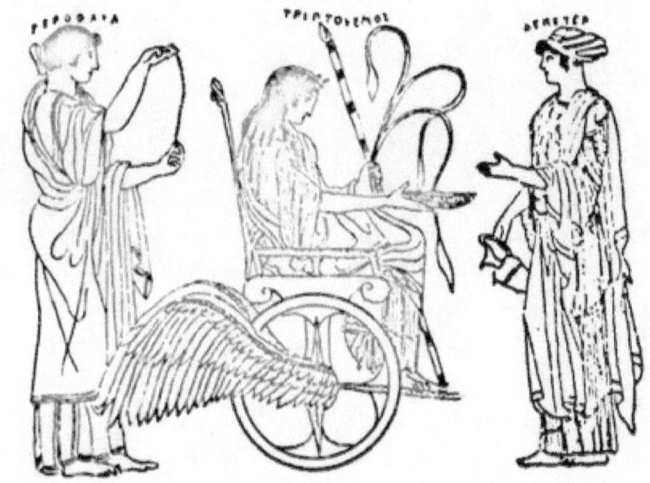

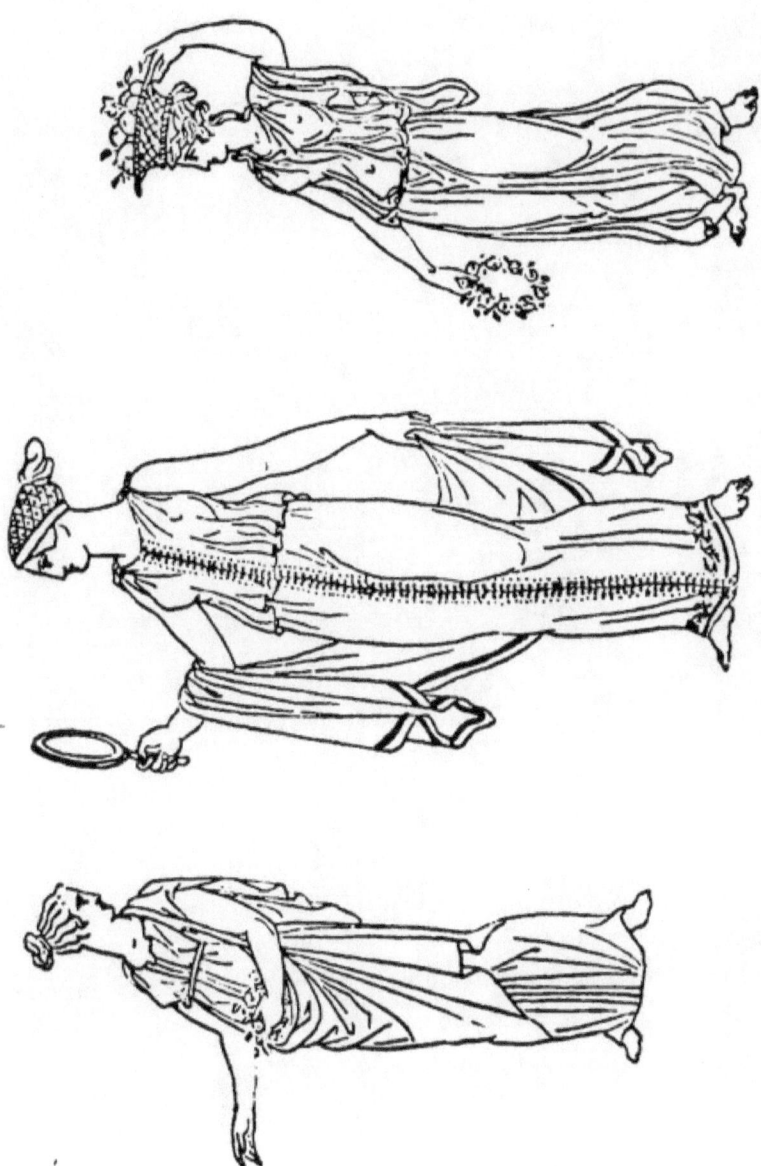

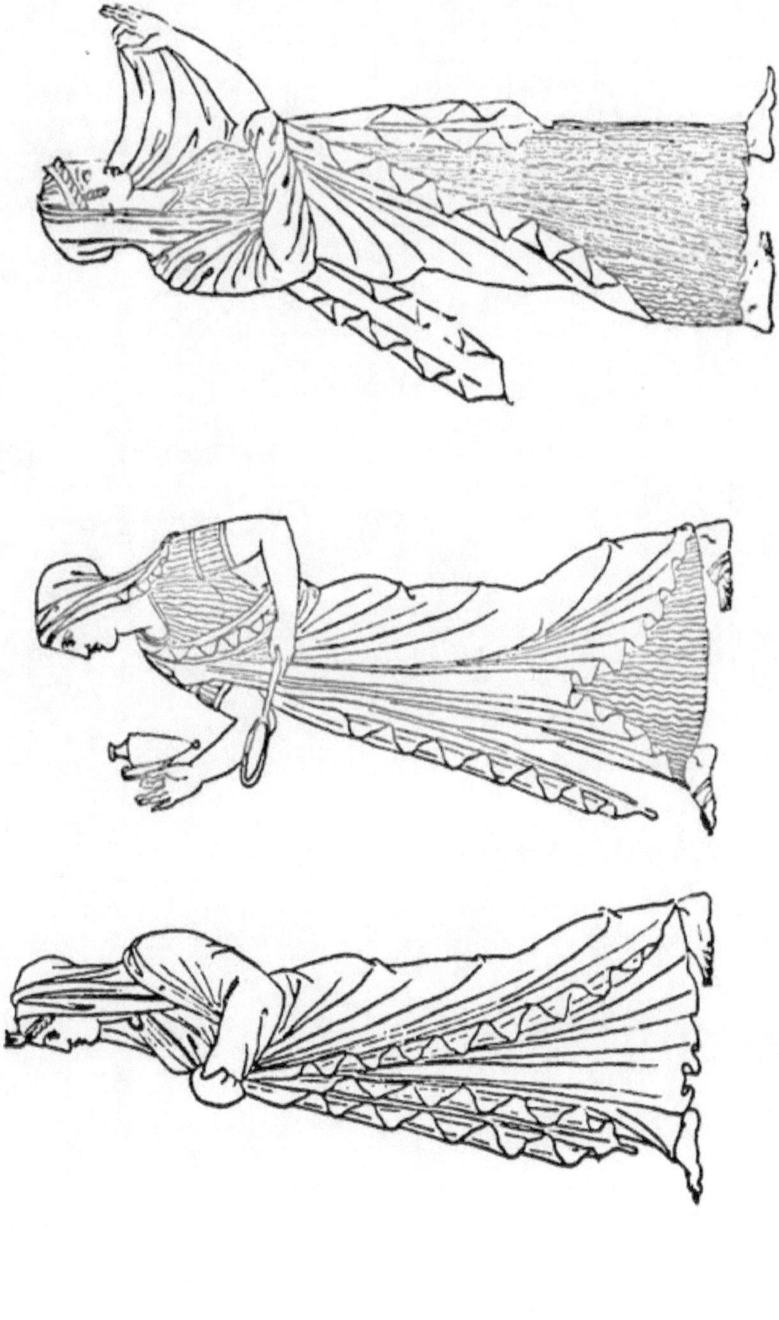

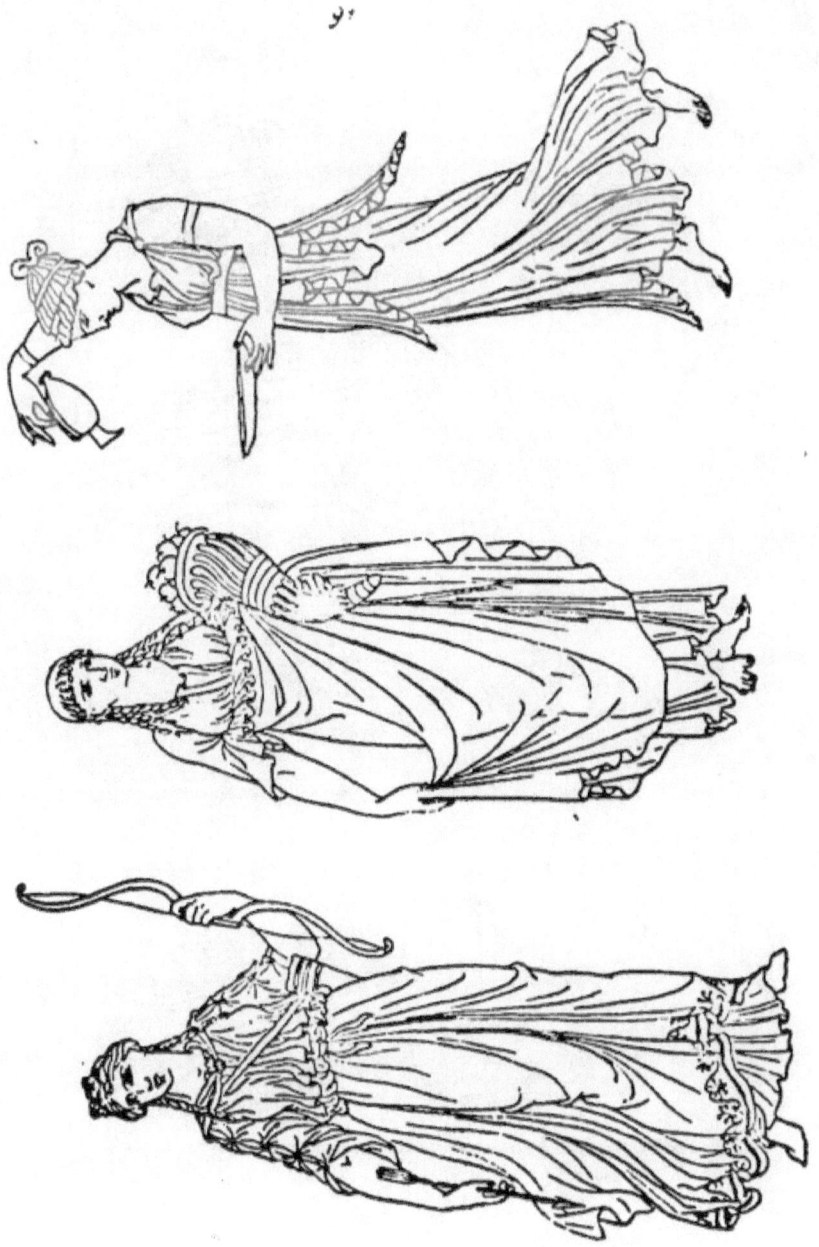

52

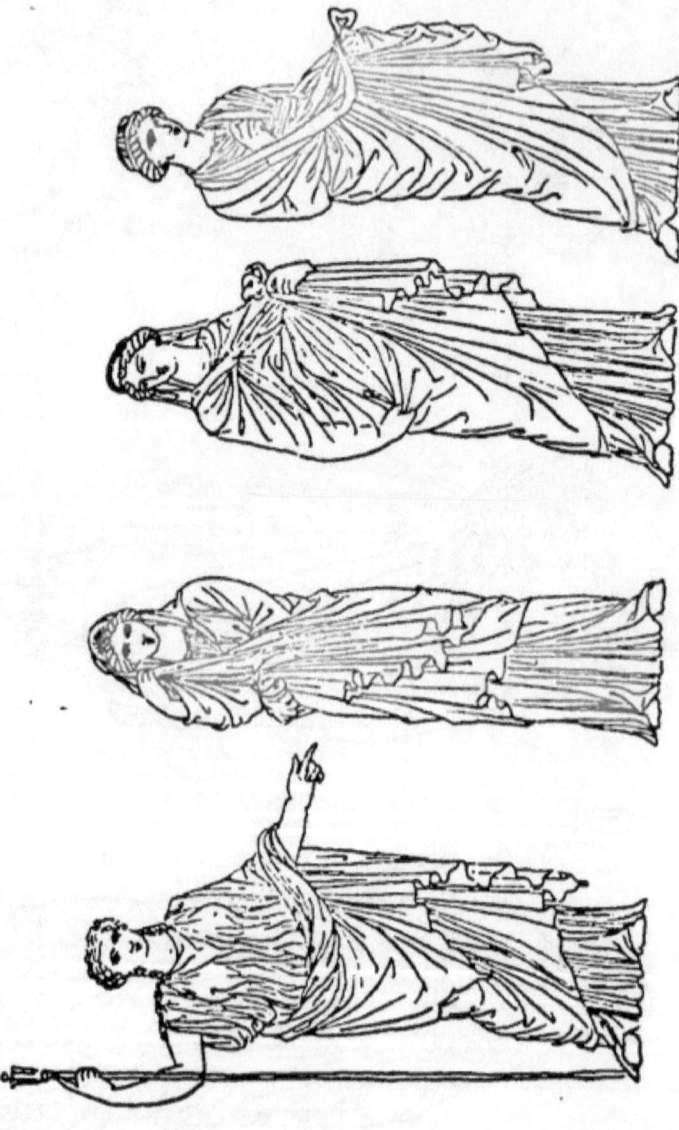

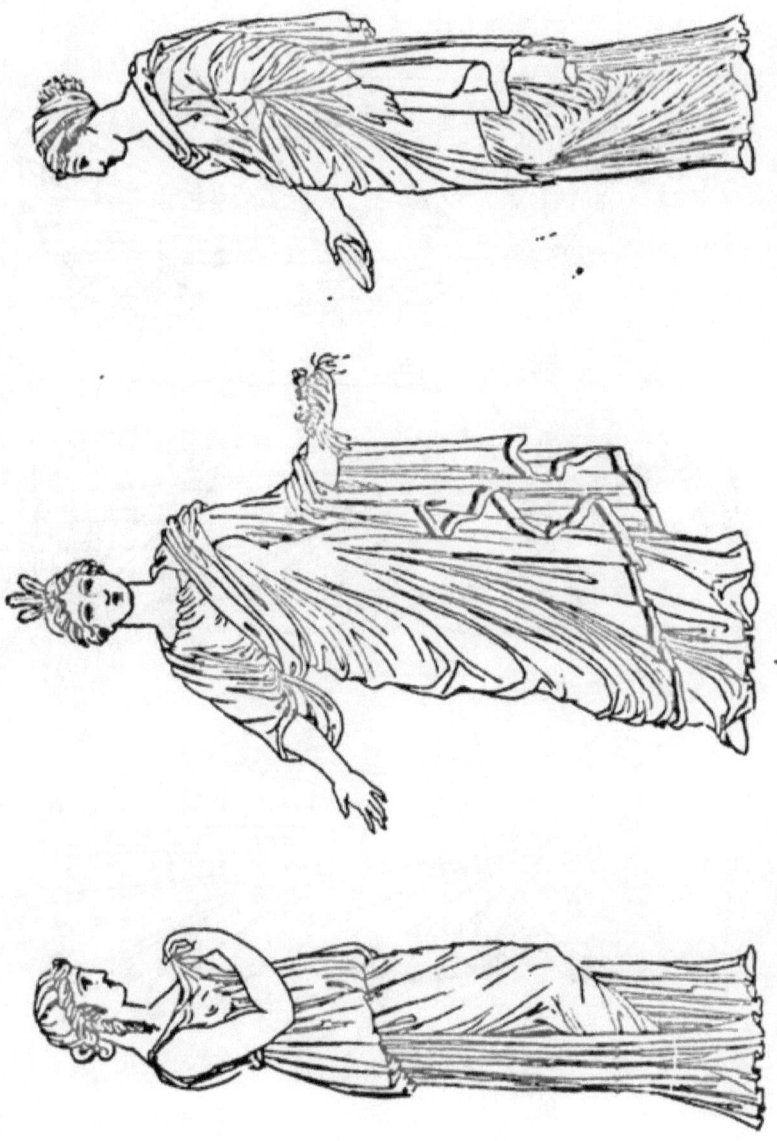

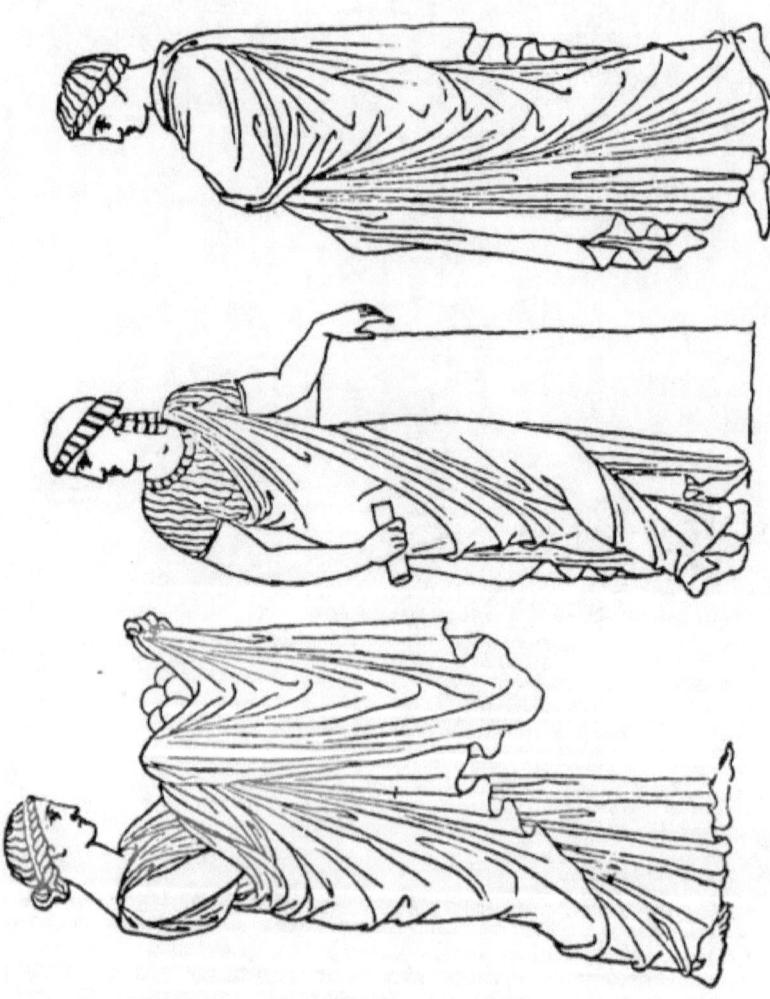

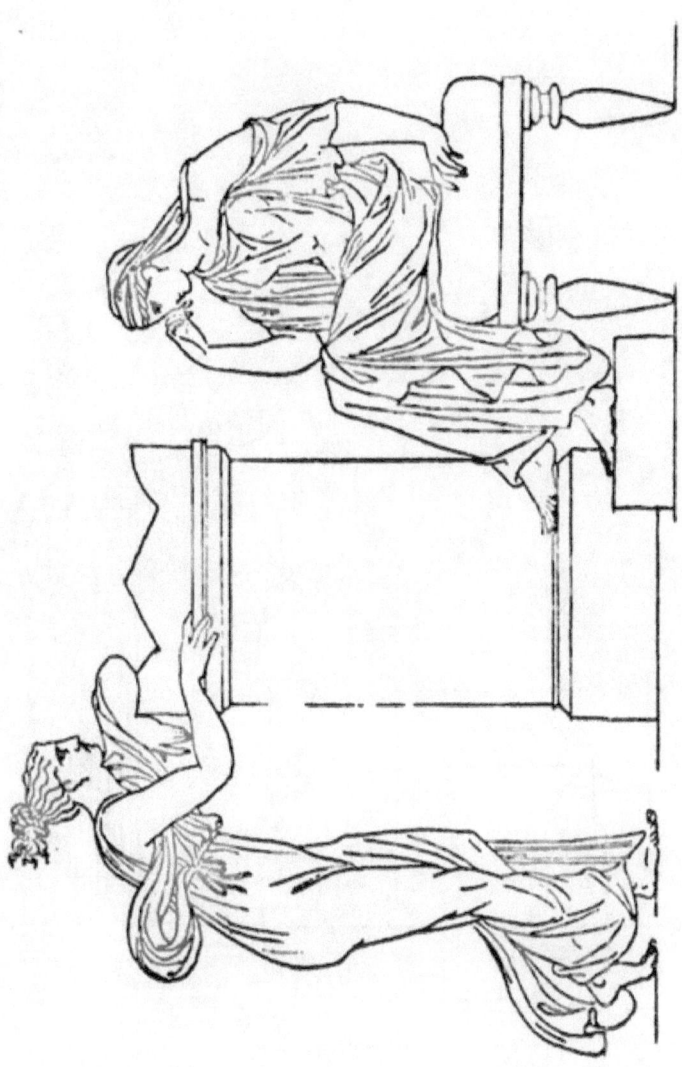

95.

99

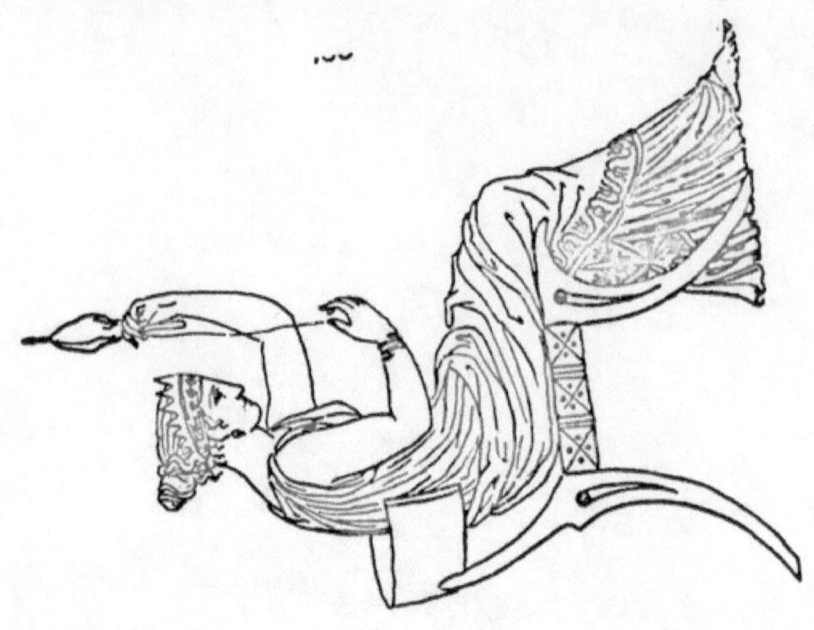

101.
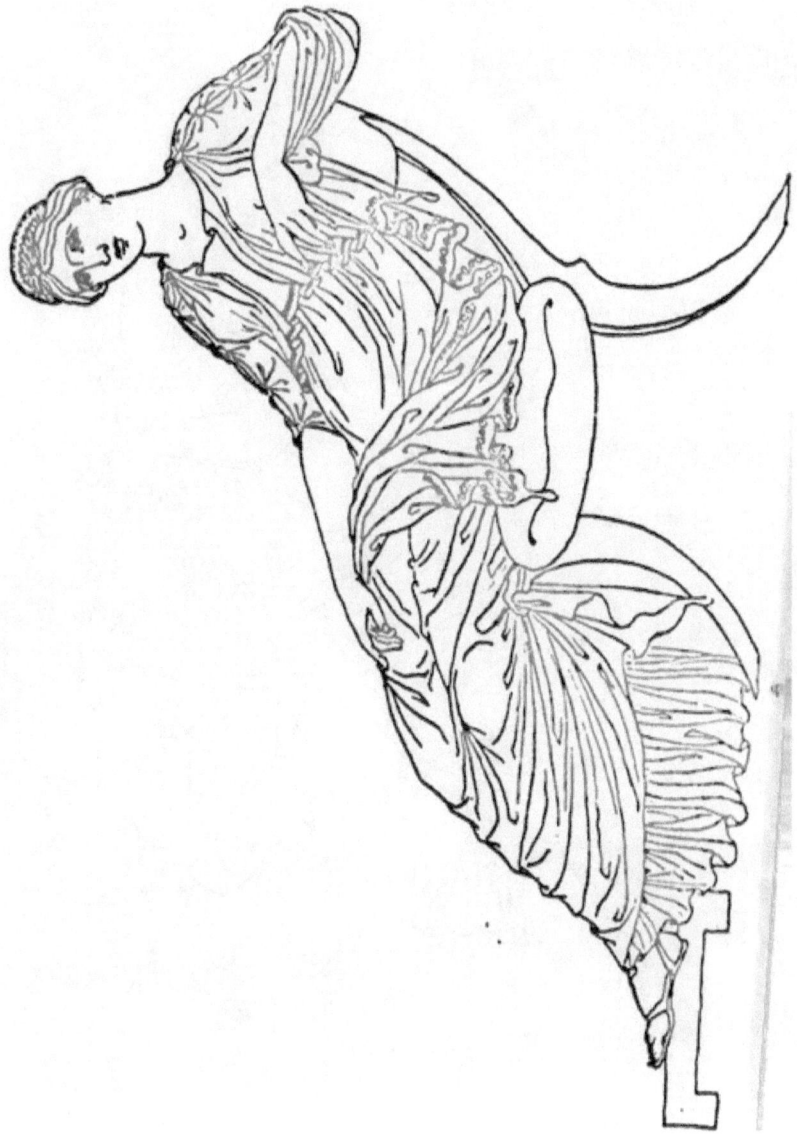

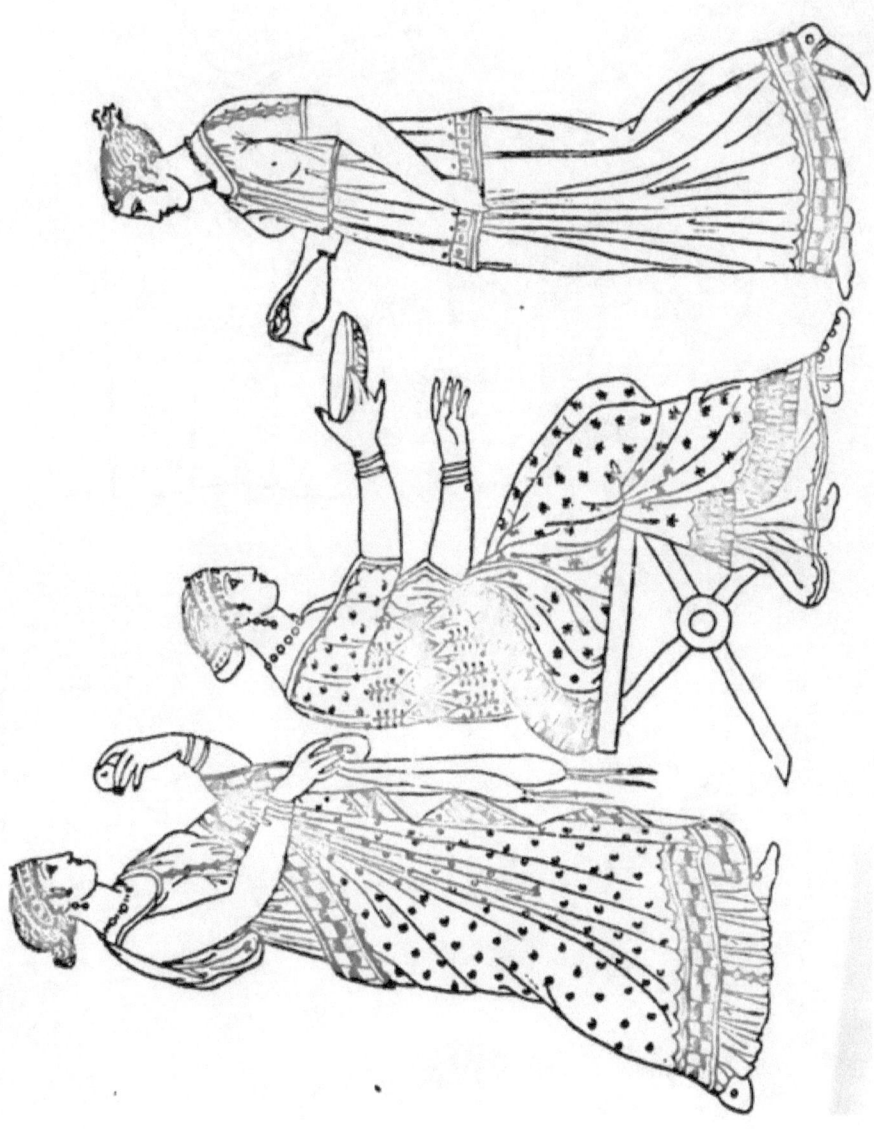

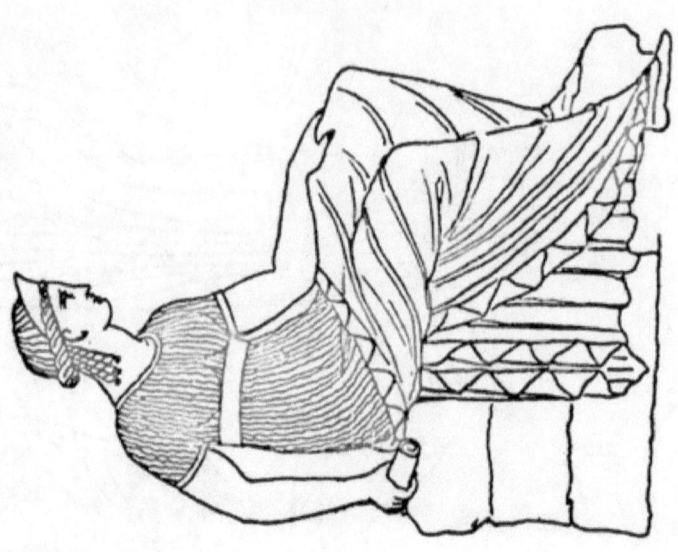

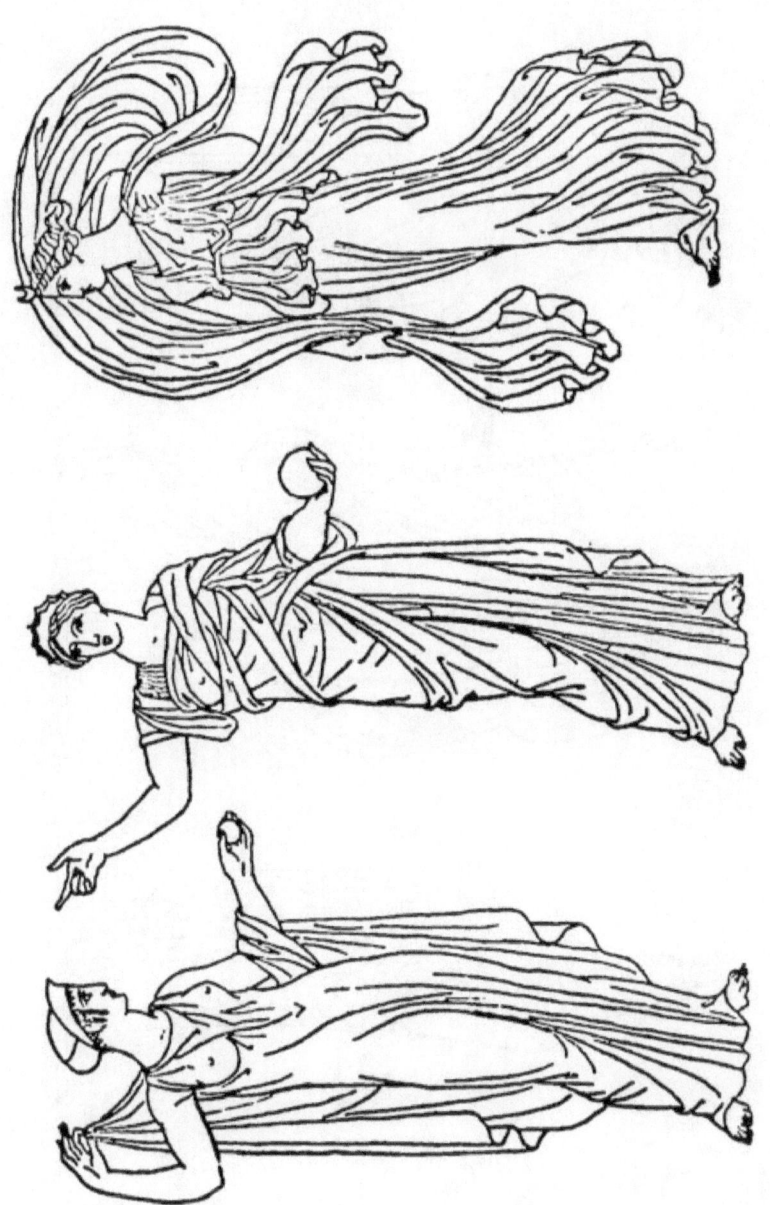

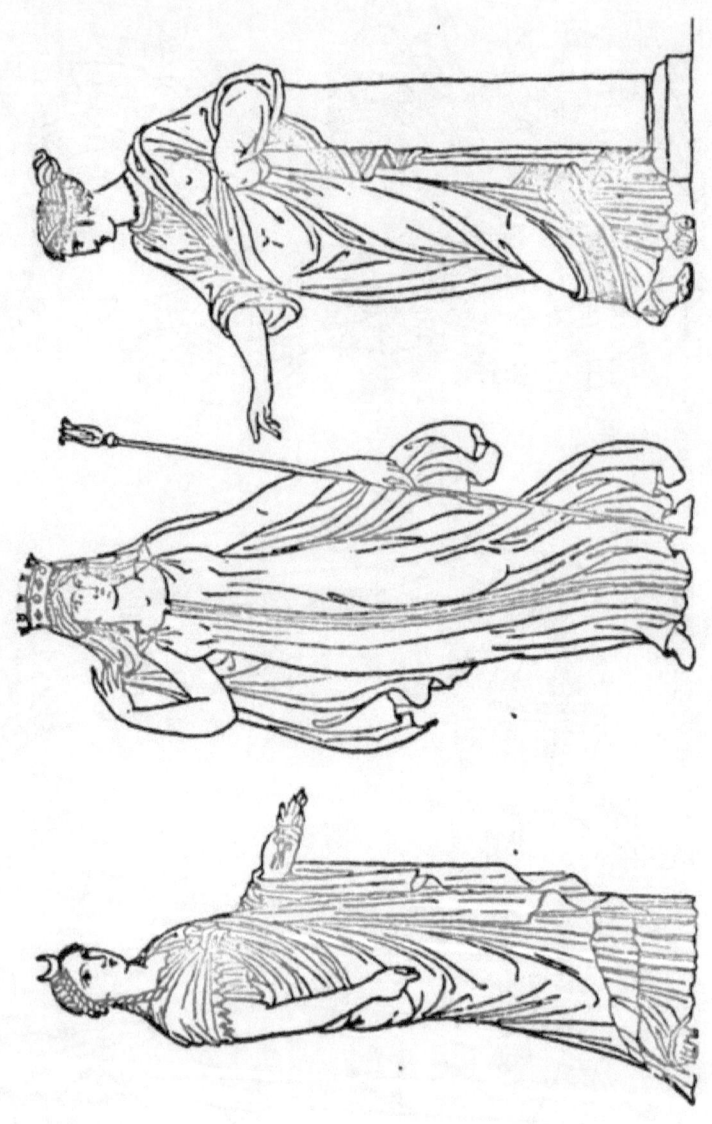

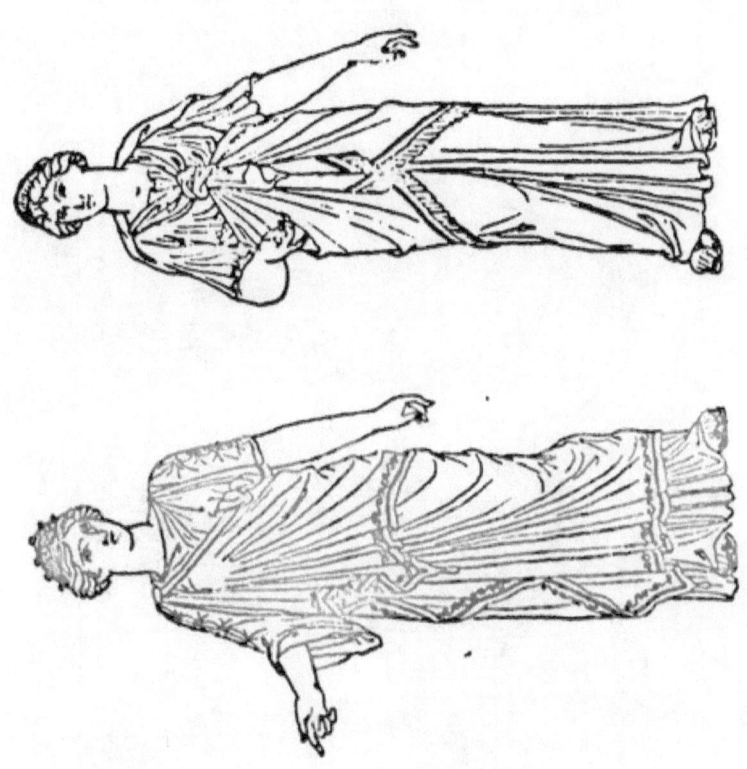

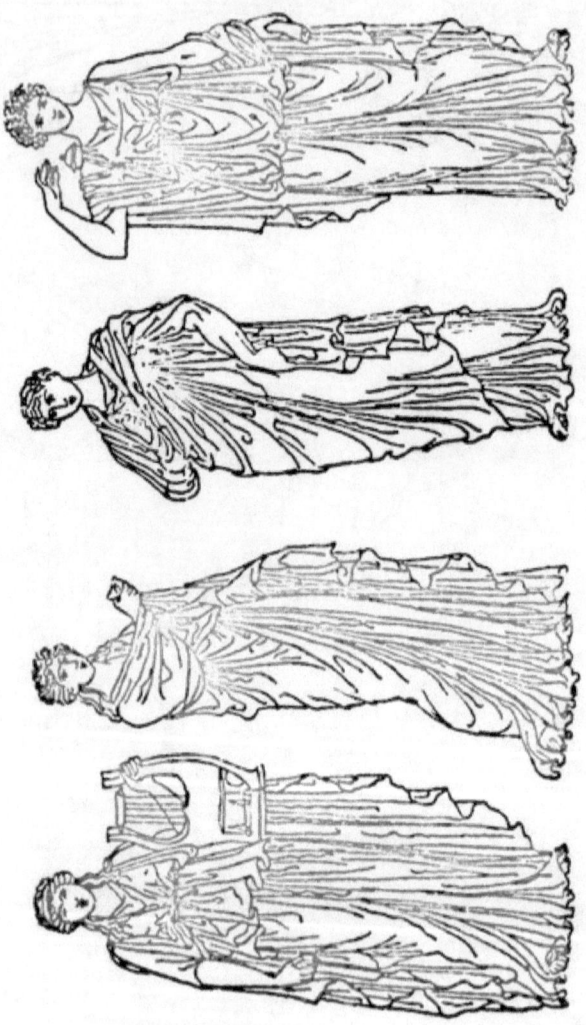

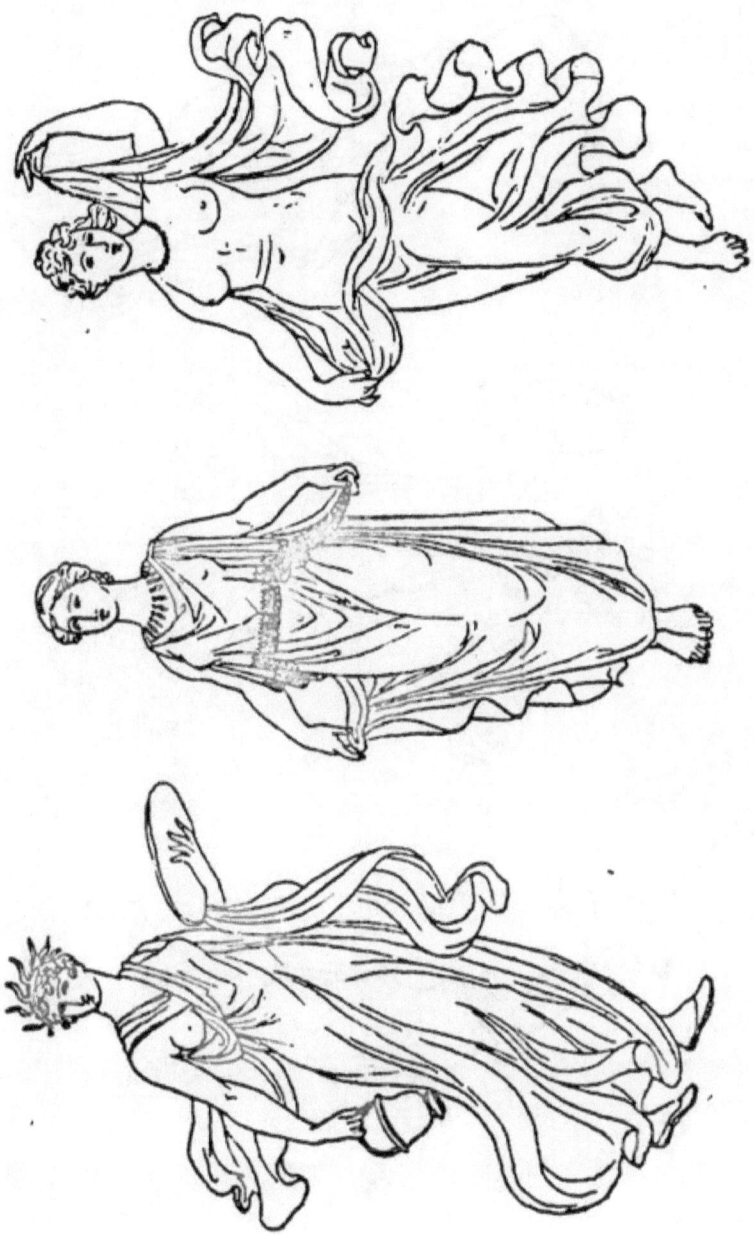

www.ingramcontent.com/pod-product-compliance
Lightning Source LLC
Chambersburg PA
CBHW032057220426
43664CB00008B/1035